Seeking His Fellowship

Seeking His Fellowship

By
Chaplain Ted L. Warmack, D.D.

DayStar
Publishing

PO Box 464 Miamitown, Ohio 45041

PUBLISHER'S NOTE
Scripture quotations are from the text
of the Authorized King James Version
of the Bible. Any deviations are not
intentional

1st Printing March 2010

Library of Congress Control Number
2010927193
ISBN 978-1-890120-30-6

Dedication

This book is dedicated to my Christian family...every blood bought sinner in this world saved by the finished work of our Savior, the Lord Jesus Christ. May it encourage, uplift and edify as you seek the Light of His Fellowship while together we look ... *"for that Blessed hope, and the glorious appearing of the great God and our Saviour Jesus Christ;"* Titus 2:1 3

Contents

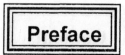

Preface

The need for this book, *Seeking His Fellowship*, was one that burned in my heart for quite some time before the Lord finally impressed upon me to write it. Although *"fellowship with Jesus Christ"* is, by far, the most important aspect of the Christian life, there are far too few authors willing to tread this subject's pathway. I believe this to be the most neglected subject in Christianity today, not only by writers, but also in our churches as well. This should not be!

Of the several books I have perused on this subject, most were beneficial. Some were entertaining and some spiritually inviting, while others were eloquently written and a few had nuggets to be gleaned by the reader.

The main focus of these covered: the need for, the benefits of, along with the joy, fulfilment and spiritual fruit of a close relationship with the Lord. But, unfortunately, few ventured to set parameters for a course to get there; or offer an antidote for the snares and pitfalls sure to be set by the host of Hell along the way.

Naturally, any discourse on a divine fellowship between God and man can be a wonderful thing to read about and on which to contemplate. However, for anyone seeking the *Light of His Fellowship,* there is much more direction needed for the actual journey. We have attempted to help fill that need by suggesting a course to pursue and by exposing some tools used by the powers of darkness to hinder success in this endeavor.

This work borrows considerably from the author's previous work *"The Bread Of Life" Bible Believer's Fundamental Study Course* published in 2002. Some pertinent chapters are used and augmented with new ones for the subject of *"Seeking His Fellowship."* We do not claim this to be an exhaustive work on the subject nor the only road to get there. **The only perfect work on this subject is the infallible, written word of God, the Holy Bible.**

We do claim it to be a simple practical work, applicable to the Christian's everyday life in today's world. The intent of *"Seeking His Fellowship,"* is to inspire the Christian to seek that place of fellowship near to the heart of God and then to offer some direction on how to achieve that goal.

The spiritual condition of the modern church and Christians will be revealed, and the major *"Fellowship killers,"* around which you must circumnavigate in your pursuit of Him will be exposed. Then, suggestions will be given to aid in preparing the outer man for the inward growth.

You will find that fellowship with Him while living in a lost and dying world will be no easy task, especially at first. However, the labors and sacrifices made along the way will pale in light of the blessings and rewards gained.

The guidelines and suggestions in this book will work for most. They worked for me and many others and they will work for you; if you are serious in you quest to seek Him. May the Lord Jesus Christ bless you as you seek the Light and the fullness of His fellowship.

Chapter 1

The Desire of God's Heart

And God said, "Let us make man in our image, after our likeness: and let them have dominion over the fish of the sea, and over the fowl of the air, and over the cattle, and over all the earth, and over every creeping thing that creepeth upon the earth." Gen. 1:26

As we know from the Bible, God is a Spirit with no beginning and no end. The Bible says in Ps. 90:2, *"Before the mountains were brought forth, or ever thou hast formed the earth and the world, even from everlasting to everlasting, thou art God."*

This God-Spirit wanted companionship....someone whom He could love and fellowship with. So, first He created a new dimension, the physical realm. *"In the beginning God created the heaven and the earth."* How did He do this?? *"...And the Spirit of God moved upon the face of the waters. And God said, Let there be.."* (Gen. 1:1-3)

And just like that, God spoke into existence: the earth, sun, moon, stars, and the planets, and then He created man. *"So God created man in his own image, in the image of God created he him; male and female created he them."* (Gen.1:27) With the physical realm then created, God rested.

Then, God created man in His own image with a higher

1

intelligence than the animals. Why? Because of His desire to fellowship with man *in the Spirit* and to **have man love Him as unconditionally and as passionately as He loves us that we may "walk in the Light" together.** It began in the garden of Eden.

Adam and Eve were created pure and sinless (but with a free will) to begin this walk with the Lord in the garden, but they soon fell from grace. That original fellowship (along with eternal life) was lost through sin, and now man must be born again of the Spirit (John 3) to restore that eternal life. To that end, the Lord Jesus Christ came to earth to suffer, bleed and die for sinful man. As a result, man's sin debt was paid and offered as a free gift to all who will receive it. For this cause, He now draws all men to himself for salvation. *"And I, if I be lifted up from the earth, will draw all men unto me."* John 12:32 (See also John 6:44)

However, there are many, who although drawn by the Savior Himself, still reject the Light and die in their sins. **Be honest, and if you are one of these or just not sure of your salvation, turn to the last page and take care of that before proceeding.**

And be not conformed to this world: but be ye transformed by the renewing of your mind, that ye may prove what is that good, and acceptable, and perfect, will of God. Rom. 12:2

Those who have already received the free gift of salvation should rebuke worldliness and, *"Draw nigh to God, and he will draw nigh to you...."* James 4:8. This is God's will. He is waiting on you to begin "walking in the light" of His fellowship, but that means more than just being saved as we will explain later. But first, let's examine why this term "walking in the light" is so unfamiliar to most Christians.

Leaving God Out

It is sad that in today's times people leave God out of their life, even saved people. The majority of God's people are more concerned with desires of the flesh and the things of this world than with seeking that spiritual walk and fellowship that God longs to have with them.

In short, these carnal Christians have forfeited fellowship with God for the things of this world and the alluring lust and pride of the flesh. We were warned about this in I John 2:15. *"Love not the world, neither the things that are in the world. If any man love the world, the love of the Father is not in him. [16] For all that is in the world, the lust of the flesh, and the lust of the eyes, and the pride of life, is not of the Father, but is of the world. [17] And the world passeth away, and the lust thereof: but he that doeth the will of God abideth for ever."*

Then there are others, who at some point in their Christian life enjoyed that close fellowship but now have drifted away. And yet more who are unaware of the need for, and the way to, that close fellowship union for lack of it being taught in their churches.

Know this: God's heart's desire is to have a daily walk and communion with you "in the Spirit."

This lack of individual fellowship with the One who lives within has created an escalating void in our churches leaving them

3

Spiritually cold, worldly and commericalized. Man is now leading in place of God. What a poor substitute that is!!

Although many realize something is missing in their church, as well as from their own Christian lives, without proper spiritual guidance they pursue the wrong course to find it. A large number of God's people long for that missing element and are searching...usually in the wrong places or for the wrong thing. Some fall away and return to the world backslidden. Others gravitate to the apostate churches that replace the Holy Ghost with emotion and fast beat music to move the people. Emotion and a good feeling are not worship nor even fellowship with God. Again, a poor substitute for the real thing!

I have run across a few Christians who, in their search, are afraid they have yet to receive the Holy Ghost as if it is something that comes apart from salvation. **Actually, all who are saved are born of the Spirit** (John 3:6) and are therefore indwelt with the Holy Ghost (Rom. 8:9) at the time of salvation. However, all one has to do is look around at Christians today to know that even though they are indwelt with the Holy Ghost, most are certainly not <u>filled</u> with the Spirit. They are saved, but "luke warm" (Rev. 3:14-16) in their relationship to God.

One problem is that some misunderstand the position and work of the Spirit and put more emphasis on Him than on the Lord Jesus Christ. This is a terrible error. The believer should understand the reason the Holy Ghost was sent: **1)** To give us power. *"But ye shall receive power, after that the Holy Ghost is come upon you: and ye shall be witnesses unto me both in Jerusalem, and in all Judaea, and in Samaria, and unto the uttermost part of the* *earth."* Acts 1:8

2) To testify of Jesus Christ: *"But when the Comforter is come, whom I will send unto you from the Father, even the Spirit of truth, which proceedeth from the Father, he shall <u>testify of me</u>:* John 15:26

3) To glorify Jesus Christ, not Himself: *Howbeit when he, the Spirit of truth, is come, he will guide you into all truth: for he <u>shall not speak of himself</u>; but whatsoever he shall hear, that shall he speak: and he will shew you things to come. [14] <u>He shall glorify me</u>:* John 16:13-14   Let's get the order right.

Seeking Him

Your focus should be on the Lord Jesus Christ and seeking His fellowship through the power and guidance of the Holy Ghost. This is the right road to victory. So, understand that there is nothing in this life more important to the born again child of God than his or her personal relationship with the Lord Jesus Christ. Fellowship, by definition, is *a close and mutually agreed on companionship,* and in this case, it is the secret of a victorious Christian life. Hopefully, that is your goal.

If so, your desire for this relationship will be greatly enhanced by your understanding of His immeasurable love for you. Outside of His dying for your sins, nothing illustrates that love better than the following verse: *Behold, what manner of love the Father hath bestowed upon us, that we should be called the sons of God: therefore the world knoweth us not, because it knew him not. [2] Beloved, now are we the sons of God, and it doth not yet appear what we shall be: but we know that, when he shall appear, we shall be like him; for we shall see him as he is. [3] And every man that hath this hope in him purifieth himself, even as he is pure.* I John 3:1-3

Imagine that! He not only suffered and died for your sins but also that you may have a way to defeat death and Hell through Him. He made you a son, sanctified you and set you apart from the world, and promised you a likeness like Him! (See also Phil. 3:21, Eph. 5:30) This infinite love is the doorway to that fellowship you seek. Come, He is waiting on you!

One doesn't have far to go to make contact because He lives within us! Simply reach out. Spiritually, His hand is already extended in fellowship waiting on you. Once connected, the infinite journey begins. Now along with the growth of that relationship comes an inner joy and manifestation of spiritual fruits that few of today's Christians ever experience. A

> **God is faithful, by whom ye were called unto the fellowship of his Son Jesus Christ our Lord.** I Cor. 1:9

return like giving! *"A good measure, pressed down, and shaken together, and running over of love, joy, peace, longsuffering, gentleness, goodness, faith, meekness, and temperance."*

These are all good reasons why you should seek and maintain His presence in your day to day routine and why this endeavor should surpass all else in purpose and intensity throughout your day. This fulltime fellowship with God is hardly a priority with most Christians. However, good things will begin to happen once you make the commitment and begin.

6

Then again, starting the journey is one thing, while staying the course is yet another. Progression and growth in this relationship will come only through your total surrender to Him and to His will in your life, as you continually seek Him within, and "walk in the Light" daily. It will not be easy, especially at first. Why?

Because it is difficult to give up our own will and to submit to His, but this must be done. Your spiritual growth will come that way or it will not come. However, know that the reward will be great and the new relationship will be an ongoing adventure that will change your life forever. One of the greatest rewards will be the element of personal communication with Him.

Have you ever heard some Christian say, "God told me" or "God spoke to me" and wondered what in the world they were talking about? Although God gets the blame for many messages that never came from Him, this could, and does really happen with Spirit filled Christians.

> *"If ye abide in me, and my words abide in you, ye shall ask what ye will, and it shall be done unto you. 8 Herein is my Father glorified, that ye bear much fruit; so shall ye be my disciples"*
> John 15:7-8

Note however, that one has to be careful here to try the spirits as you are instructed in I John 4:1: *"Beloved, believe not every spirit, but try the spirits whether they are of God: because many false prophets are gone out into the world."* If it contradicts the Bible, it is not God's Spirit speaking. Eventually, you will learn to recognize His voice speaking to your heart. **To enjoy such a relationship with the creator of the universe is immensely**

7

satisfying and eternally rewarding.

So, imagine being able to communicate with Him in the Spirit and receive guidance for the issues of daily life! Yes, He does want to be involved in your daily routine, and yes, God <u>will</u> communicate with you by speaking to your heart! You will learn to recognize His "voice," which is the manifestation of a spiritual fellowship flowing between the heart of God and you!

You will find that He does a much better job of running your life than you have in the past! This is God's desire. Should it not be yours as well? You can, and should, turn to Him on bended knees right now and make your commitment to seek that relationship.

Understand, however, that it will take more than the meager efforts and uncertain course of the average Christian. For one to pray, study, know the Bible well, attend and serve in the Church regularly, is <u>commendable</u>, and even a <u>vital</u> part of *"walking in the Light."* However, that effort alone does not guarantee the close spiritual walk God desires for us.

The churches are full of born again believers who are out of fellowship with God and don't even realize it. There is only one road to fellowship and it is paved with a repentant heart! You must abide in Him first for your efforts of service to bear sound fruit.

Why? Because it's not about service or your efforts in the energy of the flesh, nor what you do or accomplish for Him. It's about a full time fellowship and communion with Him. This is the

catalyst for that personal relationship and a springboard to serving
<u>out of a love commitment</u> rather than out of a feeling of
obligation.

Get the motive right!
Then you will
advance above the
old feeling many
have of, *"I know I'm
in a good Bible
believing church, but
I just can't get
excited about going
to Church, or*

> *Abide in me, and I in you. As the
> branch cannot bear fruit of itself,
> except it abide in the vine; no more
> can ye, except ye abide in me. [5] I am
> the vine, ye are the branches: He that
> abideth in me, and I in him, the same
> bringeth forth much fruit:* **for without
> me ye can do nothing.** John 15:4-5

praying, or serving the Lord. Or, *"I just don't know why I am not
more excited about the Lord...why don't I love to read and study
my Bible more than I do?* Etc. etc. etc.

It is simply a matter of you making fellowship with Him your top
priority. Then, if you are truly seeking His face, be assured that
once you are securely in the mode of *walking in the Light,* you
will hunger for Bible knowledge like never before. Your prayer
life will take on new dimensions, and you will covet fellowship
with your church brethren like never before. If you don't have
that attitude now, maybe it's time to evaluate your own condition
with respect to fellowship with God. Where are you now? Do
you truly abide in Him? Where would you really like to be in your
relationship with Him? Assuming you want it to be the best it
can be, let's consider what this fellowship is really like.

First of all, it is not simply a higher plateau to be attained and then rest or stop. But rather, it is a living, growing, infinite relationship. It is one that manifests the fruits of the Spirit and brings the peace and confidence of knowing that He is near in one's life and much more.

Where this closeness ultimately goes will depend on you and the level to which you seek take it. Therefore, a simple description is elusive and hard to put into words but we find some good examples in the Bible.

A Look At Fellowship

As we ponder the various aspects of fellowship with God (either spiritual or physical) some Biblical examples come to mind. In the physical realm, Adam and Eve immediately stand out in our thoughts.

Try to picture them walking in the cool of the day with the Lord in the Garden of Eden before being separated from Him by sin. What an experience that must have been to have their Maker literally by their side! Then, what a devastating loss they must have suffered upon realizing that by their own hands the relationship had been forfeited due to simple disobedience.

Consider also Enoch who walked with God (Gen. 5:24) so closely that God just translated him out of the physical world into the spiritual realm! Also, later in time, the Lord Himself chose to return to the physical realm as baby Jesus and to grow up among man, who He had created (John1:3). Then, as He grew into adulthood and His ministry progressed, picture the divine fellowship that took root and flourished between Jesus and His apostles.

Imagine those trusted companions (except for Judas) being with Him and witnessing the awesome power of God in the flesh (I Tim. 3:16) as He healed the sick, made the blind to see, enabled the lame to walk and even raised the dead.

> *And without controversy great is the mystery of godliness: God was manifest in the flesh, justified in the Spirit, seen of angels, preached unto the Gentiles, believed on in the world, received up into glory.* I Tim. 3:16

Surely in awe, they saw Him control the mighty winds, make the turbulent sea calm and even walk on the troubled water.

And, what a joy it must have been, realizing in their hearts who He really was and with whom they had the privilege to be with.

> *Jesus saith unto him, "Have I been so long time with you, and yet hast thou not known me, Philip? he that hath seen me hath seen the Father; ...."* John 14:9

The picture this fellowship presents is profound, and will remain unmatched in the physical realm until Christ returns for a glorious reunion with His Church in the air! (I Thess. 4:17)

Then, visualize when they retired from public scrutiny to rest in some remote spot in the cool of the day. In the quietness and peacefulness of that retreat, what an incredible fellowship must have ensued, as they relaxed and conversed with Him!

See in your mind's eye, John the beloved disciple as his head lay on the breast of Jesus (John 13:23-25) at supper. **A head resting**

within inches of the heart of the living God (mere inches from eternal life!) **and Creator of the universe, as He lay there miraculously manifested in the flesh,** (John 1:14, I Tim. 3:16).

He was so near to a heart that with every beat pumped God's own blood (Acts 20:28) through the veins and arteries of the God-man who came solely to suffer, bleed and die that you might have eternal life through His sacrifice. How could anyone not desire fellowship with One who loved him so? Moreover, how could one not hunger to serve Him and please Him?

Furthermore, what thoughts must have been going through John's mind at such a time? We know that Jesus loved all His disciples (John 13:1-2), but John was special (John 20:2)! Why was John special to the heart of Jesus? Although John had a great capacity for truth and spiritual insight, undoubtably it was John's exceptional love <u>for</u> Jesus! Pure love begat pure love in return! What an absolutely indescribable closeness and fellowship John must have felt with the Lord Jesus Christ!

By what means could we possibly measure such fellowship? This was fellowship beyond comprehension without having the experience yourself!

It is simply impossible for us to understand those emotions without having been there among them and having been a part of that experience. Would you, my Christian friend, like such an experience? Yes, it is possible, although in a different way in this present day!

While this physical fellowship is not possible today, we **can**, and

should, still seek it's equal in the **spiritual realm**. And although different, it can be just as miraculous of an experience for you as the physical experience was for them. It can be as fulfilling and wonderful as it was for John, maybe even more so. After all, the Spirit of the Living God now living inside of you (if you are saved) has unlimited power to work in your life! **Since He dwells inside, that is where the fellowship must begin and grow. When He speaks to you that voice will come from the Spirit within directly to your heart!**

The course of that growth can be likened to a vessel being formed at the potter's wheel to the potter's liking. The Christian also must be a vessel surrendered to the cutting, molding and shaping to perfection by the hand of the Master Potter. But, how many are willing to surrender to that process? Are you? If you are, this book will help you overcome the snares and pitfalls of this life in the flesh and draw closer to the Lord Jesus Christ, as you come to know Him better than you ever have before.

There is no perfect roadmap to get there, as God deals with people differently. However, there are some basic fundamentals that are common to all. We will address some of these to establish direction. To that end, some recommendations will be made in the final chapter in an attempt to steer you in the right direction to achieve your goal. However, you don't need to skip what is in between!

Those chapters will be the foundation on which you can begin building a victorious relationship by *living and walking in the light.* You will find little company in this endeavor simply because it is not taught in most churches. **Oh, some give it lip**

service, but when all is said and done, there is more said than done with respect to this subject!

Consequently, in these last days it is sad indeed that *walking in the light* of His fellowship and spending their daily lives in His presence is a foreign concept to the majority of God's people. How did His Church get to this point and stray so far away from the desire of God's heart?

If chapter one has pricked your heart about *"Seeking His Fellowship,"* or simply about advancing from where you presently stand, there is a considerable foundation to lay for a successful journey.

With that in mind, it is necessary that we review the problems that brought the body of Christ to this point of being outside of fellowship with Him. As we do that in the next chapter, the Christian should examine themself in light of what has happened to the Church as a whole and avoid becoming entangled in the same web of mistakes in their personal relationship with the Lord. Or, in the event you already have, you will see the way out. Let's have a look at that.

Now this next chapter is not going to be pretty, but it is the truth and the reader needs to hear it. If thus far this book has lead you into a spiritual mood and a longing to "Seek His Fellowship" then this chapter may be somewhat depressing. It should be. When you finish you will understand how the Church fell to where it now stands, and how to avoid the same mistakes in your own Christian life. However, just bear with us, and we will guide you back to the light!

14

Chapter 2

What Went Wrong?

" I know thy works, that thou art neither cold nor hot: I would thou wert cold or hot. So then because thou art lukewarm, and neither cold nor hot, I will spue thee out of my mouth." Rev. 3:15-16

Since around 1900, the church (body of Christ) has drifted away from God and the core values of God's written Word that once made it strong. If you want the plain, simple truth, most Christians are lukewarm, even backslidden, in their relationship to Jesus Christ and His written word. This was not God's plan and far from the God - man relationship for which He created us. What happened? How have so many that genuinely love the Lord, faithfully attend church and live clean, become estranged from their Savior some without even realizing it?

How did this come about? What is the problem? It is incredibly simple. There is no spiritual power in most of today's churches because the Bible (including it's instructions on fellowship) is not being taught as it should be, or it is being mistaught. Thus, there is no genuine hunger for the written word of God. Christians by and large simply haven't been taught the need for, or directed to, a path of oneness and fellowship with Christ. Neither do people, including most Christians, fear God anymore.

The consequence of all this is that, when you mention: *"walking in the Spirit," "walking in the Light,"* or *"living daily in God's presence,"* most professing Christians have no idea what you are talking about, much less how to achieve it. This spiritual blindness has set the Church wandering aimlessly about in a fog of <u>emotionalism and materialism.</u> To elaborate further:

The average modern church goer is looking for an "emotional experience" and a good time rather than a genuine worship service and learning adventure. The church pastor is expected to entertain the congregation so they can "have

> **God's Church has become rich and increased with goods, but is Spiritually poor!**

a good time" and leave feeling like they "received a blessing."

Therefore, many pastors frantically scurry about trying to find something new and different to feed their sheep to keep them content. The main source of power in the Christian's life (the Bible) has taken a back seat to entertainment. No Bible, No power! *"For the word of God is quick, and powerful, and sharper than any twoedged sword, piercing even to the dividing asunder of soul and spirit, and of the joints and marrow, and is a discerner of the thoughts and intents of the heart."* Heb. 4:12

An emotional "feel good" service has replaced the once Holy Ghost Spirit-filled service. The real thing has been replaced by the counterfeit!

The Church is one called out body of born again believers who's charge is to walk in the light (I John 1:7), spread the Gospel of the Lord Jesus Christ (Acts 1:8), practice what they preach and bring honor and glory to Him. Instead, there is a spiritual famine in a church that has become weak and divided. In short, the Church has laid aside the Bible and has opened it's doors wide in order to welcome the world in with open arms.

> *I charge thee therefore before God, and the Lord Jesus Christ, who shall judge the quick and the dead at his appearing and his kingdom; 2 Preach the word; be instant in season, out of season; reprove, rebuke, exhort with all longsuffering and doctrine.* II Tim 4:1-2

Futher, Christians are firmly entrenched in the regiment of the Church with it's menus, schedules, order of worship, etc., which seldom leaves time or space for the work of the Holy Spirit.

Moreover, they are comfortable and unwilling to move out of their comfort zone to do the work God has bidden us to do. The call to be a soldier for Jesus Christ falls on deaf ears among the majority of Christians today. Few are " in the fight" and most are not even aware of the spiritual battle that rages between God's people and the powers of darkness. Witnessing, soul wining, and taking a stance for Christian values now takes a backseat to non spiritual secular music, emotion, and chasing of spiritual gifts and worldliness.

By and large, churches have become materialistic entertainment businesses. They are commercialized and begging for money to foot the bill for all the worldly things they considers the most important.

Pastors (and so called scholars) are paid according to the number of degrees they can claim (with the most "letters" after their name) rather than whether or not they are saved, Spirit filled men or even called by God to preach at all.

"I will spue thee out of my mouth!"Rev. 3:16

Preaching and teaching the Bible, evangelizing the community, supporting missionaries and local Bible believing ministries are largly ignored. These things are relegated to last place on the list of priorities, or they are eliminated entirely. What the churches count as the most important in these cases is the least important to God.

A Worldly Substitute

Here is another problem. A major distraction in the Christian's life and a contributor to the church's condition, is the fast pace of today's society, which is unbelievable! People run to and fro doing everything they <u>want</u> to do and have no time left to do what they <u>should</u> do. Every American is bombarded with a secular array of: sports, sex, perverted lifestyles and politics by TV, radio, and news media, to the extent they can't think for themselves anymore. A once great nation has become a "dumbed down" mundane society! God has been moved to the outside of America's door (and heart)!

America has abandoned all the values and things that made it great and swapped it for a socialistic, godless society. A nation once governed by a constitution now ignores it. Elected officals condone same sex marriage and even pass laws to make it a "hate crime" to publically call it what God called it. An abomination (Lev.18:22)! Partial birth abortion, which is simply murder, is supported by most politicians to gain votes from a secular society. This social environment has levied a great toll on the spiritual condition of God's people.

Now, as the family unit declines along with God and prayer being removed from our schools and social events, the focus is on self, education, achievments, and image. Self, number one! God is on the outside of man's heart!

It even begins at an early age. The majority of today's young people are obsessed with electronics, the flesh and their personal appearance to the point they are wearing earrings in their noses, eyes, ears, belly buttons, lips and who knows where else. They are disfiguring their bodies with tattoos in unseemly places,

Therefore hell hath enlarged herself, and opened her mouth without measure: Isa. 5:14

changing their body shape with silicone and even having plastic surgery at incredibly young ages to alter their appearance. Many have tried everything they can think of in the flesh to find peace, joy and happiness in this life, but it eludes them. It always will!

These won't come because they exist in a state of un- regenerated spiritual stagnation, lost in the worldly arena. They are outside the camp of the living God. Ditto, for the lost adults. Our country and our society has changed. We have time for self, time for the world, but no time for God. Unbelievable!

Even professing "blood bought" Christians fail to include the Lord in their daily routine in a serious,

> *".........and truly our fellowship is with the Father, and with his Son Jesus Christ.* I John 1:3

sincere, searching way. The trend is "quickie" prayers and Bible studies (if that) so the spiritually weak can get back to their wordly activities.

The Creator of the universe, the One who suffered, bled and died that we might have life and have it more spiritually abundant, is easily prioritized to Wednesday night prayer meeting and the traditional Sunday services, if even then. This was not God's plan as we mentioned earlier and hopefully is not the measure of your own relationship with Jesus Christ today. So, whatever your condition is now, if you desire a special place with Him and wish to pursue and develop that relationship, stay with us.

A Neglected Bible

Aside from a pastor's responsibility to feed the sheep (John 21:15-17), the born again child of God also has his own responsibility to study the Bible. *"Study to shew thyself approved unto God, a workman that needeth not to be ashamed, rightly dividing the word of truth."* II Tim. 2:15

God has commanded us to study so we can learn to rightly divide His written Word. Otherwise, it results in people taking doctrines that belong to an Old Testament Jew under the Law, or a Tribulation Saint, etc. and trying to apply them to the Church Age. Presto! Now the "Church " is divided into dozens of different denominations who fight over which is right! **The powers of darkness have won a major battle using this dissension to keep the lost from being saved and the saved from growing spiritually and fellowshiping with God.** We will deal more with this later.

With the miracle of all miracles and the Book of all Books, available almost anywhere, few are really interested in studying enough to learn of it's super-natural powers. In fact, most consider it a boring book. Neither do they long to hear sound Bible preaching on sin, Hell, judgment or the Christian life. Then those who **are** interested in the Book may struggle to find a faithful pastor who has studied sufficiently himself, who refuses to compromise and has the courage to preach the entire "Book!"

> *Search the scriptures; for in them ye think ye have eternal life: and they are they which testify of me.* John 5:39

The fact is, that where the Bible and sound doctrine are taught, the Holy Spirit is at work. Where it is not taught, there is no power! Without the Bible being the final authority in all matters of faith and practice, there is no meat, no bread, no milk and no honey of the word to feed God's sheep. God's people are starving and without power! Instead, a counterfeit spirit is in charge, feeding the flesh with pleasure, emotion and with worldly desires while the spirit hungers in darkness.

An Abused Bible

To make matters worse, modern scholars and pastors tend to sit in judgement of the Bible and spout their own version of what it "really means" or "should say," although God left us ample instruction **not** to change it (Deut. 4:2, Prov. 30:6, Rev. 22:18-19). His desire is for you to study it, believe it, trust it, teach it to others, and live by it.

Since the neglect of the Bible is directly connected with man's departure from God and a major factor in our subject of **"Seeking His Fellowship,"** we will look briefly at the importance scripture itself gives the written word of God.

"The words of the LORD are pure words: as silver tried in a furnace of earth, purified seven times. Thou shalt keep them, O LORD, thou shalt preserve them from this generation for ever." (Ps. 12:6-7) In this verse, we have a promise that God's words are pure and will be preserved forever! Well, where are they? With hundreds of versions available, which one has been purified seven times? It is a testimonuy to the condition of the body of Christ that this question is so widely ignored!

Which version is the one He promised to preserve? My, what a touchy subject! However, you already have the answer above! Which Bible did the Philadelphia Church Age use? Naturally, it was the only Bible the Holy Spirit has ever honored with any major work or fruit, and the only one purified through seven languages, the 1611 King James Authorized Version. Disagree? OK, then pray about it, examine the manuscript evidence and let God direct you.

* **"Where the word of a king is, there is power:"** (Eccl. 8:4)
Ours is a Jewish book authorized by a king with a Jewish name.
What is the modern Church using? You do the math! Is the Bible
really that important? Well, let's see.

* **"So then faith cometh by hearing, and hearing by the word
of God."** (Rom. 10:17) The written word (Bible) is the source of
your faith! Since faith is necessary for salvation, what value does
that verse put on your Bible? Enough to love it and study it
right?

* **"...holy scriptures, which are able to make thee wise unto
salvation through faith which is in Christ Jesus."** (II Tim. 3:15)
The Scriptures are holy and make you wise unto salvation.

* **"Being born again, not of corruptible seed, but of
incorruptible, by the word of God, which liveth and abideth
forever."** If you are saved, you were born again by the word of
God which lives forever! (I Pet. 1:23)

* **"And take the helmet of salvation, and the sword of the
Spirit, which is the word of God:"** (Eph. 6:17) God's word is our
weapon for spiritual warfare.

* **" .....for thou hast magnified thy word above all thy name"**
(Ps.138:2) He has placed it in a pretty lofty position, wouldn't
you say?

At this point I believe we have firmly established (by scripture)
that the Bible is an indispensible ingredient in one's relationship
with God and that the modern lack of focus on His Book is the

primary reason for the church's condition today. We need to get back to the old tried and true ways of God (Jer. 6:16)!

Here comes a hard, cold fact. Everyone is either a Bible believer or a Bible rejector! You can't receive only those parts you like or with which you agree. You either receive it in it's entirety, or you reject it.

This departure from the Book has ushered in an age where the individual's focus is on the flesh, life's goals and success. All of which are set and measured by man's standards rather than by God's. Therefore, people go about their everyday life in pursuit of everything but God, or at best, shift Him to the trunk as a "spare tire" to be pulled out when needed.

Now, if these descriptions of the Church as a whole today are not applicable to you or your church, praise the Lord. But are you sure? **If so, your own testimony and that of the church should bear witness to that fact.** But look around at the majority of churches today! It is obvious that the most important thing to the majority of modern day churches is to have large sanctuaries, TV screens, bands, outbuildings, busses, gyms and whatever else will entertain, impress and bring in the most people. Not that all these are bad, but there is a priority based on what the Church is called to do for Christ. Are all these more important than supporting missionaries, local evangelism and helping the poor, for example?

Welcome to the Laodicean Church Age (the last one) and it's "luke warm" lackadaisical attitude toward God and toward sound doctrine (Rev. 3:14-21)!

The instructions God left us in His Book are being ignored, thereby casting today's church into a spiritually dead ocean of apostasy. A once spiritually strong church has evolved into a luke warm church that is actually offensive to our Savior, the Lord Jesus Christ! If you doubt this, read on to see what God has to say about the last Church Age we now live in. You will be shocked!

The fruit of ignoring God's written word (the Bible) is made very clear in scripture. Consider this. The Philadelphian Church Age, from 1500-1900, (just prior to our age) was the greatest period of evangelism, revival, and missionary outreach in church history.

> **Thus saith the Lord, Stand ye in the ways, and see, and ask for the old paths, where is the good way, and walk therein, and ye shall find rest for your souls. But they said, We will not walk therein.** (Jer. 6:16)

God gave specific credit to the saints of this age in Rev. 3:8 when He said, *"..........for thou hast a little strength, and hast kept my word, and hast not denied my name"* (underline emphasis ours). It is obvious here that our Lord was pleased by those who kept His Word. There is a great lesson to be learned here as we contrast this Philadelphia ("Brotherly Love") Age with the present Age of Laodicea ("rights of the people "). To the Laodicean Age in which we now live (1900 until the Rapture), God had this to say:

"I know thy works, that thou art neither cold nor hot: I would thou wert cold or hot. So then because thou art lukewarm, and

neither cold nor hot, I will spue thee out of my mouth. Because thou sayest, I am rich, and increased with goods, and have need of nothing; and knowest not that thou art wretched, and miserable, and poor, and blind, and naked:" (Rev. 3:15-17)

What a poor testimony for today's church!! The most obvious difference, of course, is that this church grew <u>rich</u> and fell away from God and His **written word.** The church appears to be rich because of all the "things" it posesses, but God says it is poor! Moreover, it is **naked and blind** to it's condition!

It is a church rich in material things. Yet it is a church poor in the spiritual values that God's people so desperately need to bring the Church back together and to bring the individual into that inner room with God.

We can see God's reaction to the changed and weakened spiritual condition of the church due to it's <u>pursuit of riches and</u>

> *Behold, I stand at the door, and knock: if any man hear my voice, and open the door, I will come in to him, and will sup with him, and he with me.* Rev 3:20

<u>the favor of man rather than walking with Him</u>. This church thinks it is great, wonderful and Spirit-filled, but, in reality, it makes God want to puke! Today's church, like an earlier church, has left their "first love" (Rev. 2:4) and needs to return to Jesus Christ and to His written word. Power belongs to God, (I Cor. 2:5) not men, and that power is manifested through that word (Heb. 4:12).

26

Some Christians seem to think the more prosperous churches become the more spiritual they are because God must have blessed them. This is not the case because if God was in it, most of the money would go to missionaries, evangelists and local ministries spreading the gospel, rather than to the flashy buildings, property and <u>things</u>.   The truth is, they have been tested and failed the test!

God is not interested in your <u>material</u> abundance. He is interested in HIS Son, the Lord Jesus Christ, that He be honored and glorified and that the world come to know and trust Him. He is interested in the spiritual condition of His church. The power to bring that spiritual condition to fruit, is provided in His written word, the Bible, which now does little but gather dust in the church.

By now you have realized that the condition of the church today was well prophesied and should surprise no one. Understand that this is a corporate condition and not an individual one. Just because the body of Christ, as a whole, is weak and out of fellowship doesn't mean you have to be. Let's move along.

Next, it is necessary to become more familiar with the God you seek. To this end we will explore His attributes in the next chapter. After which, subsequent chapters will point out potential pitfalls along your journey. All these are necessary to prepare you for the fellowship you seek. The foundation is important because the last thing the Devil wants is for you to *walk in the Light.*

Chapter 3

Knowing God Better

"It is done. I am Alpha and Omega, the beginning and the end. I will give unto him that is athirst of the fountain of the water of life freely."
Rev. 21:6

W hat is God like? If you ask most people this question you will likely hear these answers: "God is love" or "God is a Spirit," or "God is everywhere" or "God intimidates." I have been told that He is an inspiration and a helper in time of need. Naturally, all of these answers are true, but our God has many more attributes than the average Christian realizes. Out of all the people I asked (all professing Christians) not one said "a Savior." Actually, the more Christians you ask, the more one begins to realize that even saved people know very little about their God. It seems everyone's opinion is centered around his or her own personal experience with God and in most cases, that experience itself is limited.

It is appalling that the vast majority of God's people know more about the characteristics of movie stars, TV personalities, or sports figures than they do their own God who suffered, bled and died that they may live! It is not uncommon to hear professing Christians elaborate on every detail of their favorite sports player's life, abilities and accomplishments. Ditto for many when asked about their pets or hobbies! But, ask this same person to describe the living God, and you will normally get only one or two of His many attributes in response.

This should not be! God has revealed Himself to us through His written word, through the incarnate Word, the Lord Jesus Christ and through His creation around us. Our source for this lesson will be the medium of His written word, the Bible. That way there will be no guesswork in the description of His nature and characteristics.

In Phil.3, the Apostle Paul tells us it was worth losing all to *"...know Him and the power of His ressurection."* Would that we could all have Paul's mindset! Hopefully, this chapter will help you come to know God better, so not only your understanding, but also your relationship with God will improve. Let's face it. **You simply cannot have fellowship with One you don't know!**

A Big God

Have you ever thought about how big God really is? Obviously, from Scripture we know He came as a little child and grew into a man. It is also apparent that He can manifest Himself into any size He chooses. For example: *"Mine hand also hath laid the foundation of the earth, and my right hand hath spanned the heavens: when I call unto them, they stand up together."*(Isa. 48:13)

From the size of a child in a manger to large enough that His hand can span the heavens! Do you know how large the heavens are as we are able to determine with today's science? How about 72 quintrillion light years across! Forget it! You can't even imagine how far that is! But, there is quite a contrast between a child and the size of that hand!

Note what David said in Ps. 139:8; *"If I ascend up into heaven, thou art there: if I make my bed in hell, behold, thou art there."* Quite a "span" there as well, isn't there? Or try this one: *"............Do not I fill heaven and earth? saith the Lord."* (Jer.23:24)

Suffice it to say that He is big enough that He is always wherever you are and will be there when you need Him, <u>if in fact you are one of His</u>. Remember His promise: *"....for he hath said, I will never leave thee, nor forsake thee."* (Heb. 13:5)

God is Holy

If you had to give a one word description of God, the one word that would cover the most ground would be **"holy."** God's holiness is synonymous with His other characteristics. His holiness is what separates Him from sinful man. The word "holy" means whole, sinless and spiritually pure. He is perfect! He is totally righteous!

> *"For I am the Lord your God: ye shall therefore sanctify yourselves, and ye shall be holy; for I am holy: ....."* Lev. 11:44

"There is none holy as the Lord: for there is none beside thee: neither is there any rock like our God." (1 Sam. 2:2)

He is the only purely righteous, totally sinless and perfect Being in the universe! *"... God sitteth upon the throne of his holiness."*

30

(Ps. 47:8) Not only is He holy, but all His works are holy. *"The Lord is righteous in all his ways, and holy in all his works"* (Ps. 145:17).

God expects us to be holy as He is holy. Although we could never reach the level of His holiness, we are expected to try! So, set this as your goal!

God is holy and will always be holy. *"And the four beasts had each of them six wings about him; and they were full of eyes within: and they rest not day and night, saying, Holy, holy, holy, Lord God Almighty, which was, and is, and is to come."* (Rev. 4:8) He is coming back!

God Is Righteous

God is righteous. Righteous means just, virtuous and morally right. *"O Lord God of Israel, thou art righteous: for we remain yet escaped, as it is this day: behold, we are before thee in our trespasses: for we cannot stand before thee because of this."* (Ezra. 9:15) *"His work is honourable and glorious: and his righteousness endureth for ever."* (Ps.111:3) God's righteousness goes hand in hand with His holiness. His judgments are perfect every time. He is never wrong. *"And the heavens shall declare his righteousness: for God is judge himself. Selah."* (Ps. 50:6)

God is Light

God is so righteous and pure that He is likened to light. Pure light so bright and brilliant you could not even look at it and live (Ex. 33:20). Jesus dwells in the presence and light of God the Father which no man can see or approach. *"Who only hath immortality, dwelling in the light which no man can approach unto; whom no man hath seen, nor can see: to whom be honour and power everlasting. Amen."* (I Tim. 6:16)

When Jesus, who, of course, is God's body, (I Tim. 3:16) appeared to Saul (Paul) on the road to Damascus, the light blinded Paul for three days until he was healed.

In the great city of New Jerusalem, there will be no need for the sun or moon because He will supply all the light for it!

Then spake Jesus again unto them, saying, I am the light of the world: he that followeth me shall not walk in darkness, but shall have the light of life. John 8:12

"And the city had no need of the sun, neither of the moon, to shine in it: for the glory of God did lighten it, and the Lamb is the light thereof." (Rev. 21:23) We as Christians are called "children of light," and are told not to walk in darkness. *"Ye are all the children of light, and the children of the day: we are not of the night, nor of darkness."* (I Thess. 5:5)

His light is the opposite of darkness. The Devil and his demons are likened to darkness (Eph 6:12). *"This then is the message which we have heard of him, and declare unto you, that <u>God is light, and in him is no darkness at all</u>. [7] But if we walk in the light, as he is in the light, we have fellowship one with another, and the blood of Jesus Christ his Son cleanseth us from all sin.* (I John 1:5 & 7)

The subject of this book is about walking in the light of His fellowship...... away from the darkness.

God Is Eternal

God has no beginning and no end. He **IS** the beginning and the end. This is another characteristic that is hard for our minds to conceive. One natural question would be: "If He was always here, was there anything or any other creature always here as well, or was God the only one, or thing here?" The answer is, God has always existed and He created every person, every place and every thing. We know from the Bible He was here at the very beginning, as we understand it. *"In the beginning God created the heaven and the earth."* (Gen. 1:1)

He is the past, the present and the future! *"I am Alpha and Omega, the beginning and the ending, saith the Lord, which is, and which was, and which is to come, the Almighty."* (Rev. 1:8) If there is no beginning time for God, then His

> I am Alpha and Omega, the beginning and the ending, saith the Lord, which is, and which was, and which is to come, the Almighty. Rev. 1:8

existence would be a circle of time. No beginning and no end. He is in the past, present and future all at the same time.

What we know for sure is what the word of God says. He WAS before the world was formed and WILL BE here forever! *"Before the mountains were brought forth, or ever thou hadst formed the earth and the world, even from everlasting to everlasting, thou art God."* (Ps. 90:2) His Kingdom will last forever. *"..For thine is the kingdom, and the power, and the glory, for ever."*

(Mat. 6:1)

God The Creator

"In the beginning God created the heaven and the earth." (Gen. 1:1) He is creator of the universe, of mankind, and all of things that exist, ever did exist, or ever will exist. *"In the beginning was the Word, and the Word was with God, and the Word was God. [2] The same was in the beginning with God. [3] All things were made by him; and without him was not any thing made that was made. [4] In him was life; and the life was the light of men. [5] And the light shineth in darkness; and the darkness comprehended it not."* (John 1:1-5) Jesus and God are synonymous here.

God is superior to all and all creation is subject to Him and under His control including the Devil, his angels and demons. (Job 1:6-12, I Cor. 8:5-6, Isa 14:12-17) This one single characteristic is hidden to 99.9 % of the world. They are all too busy trying to make everything happen the way they want it to with total disregard to what God <u>said</u> was going to happen! And did! And will!

Thou art worthy, O Lord, to receive glory and honour and power: for thou hast created all things, and for thy pleasure they are and were created. Rev. 4:11

Unfortunately, it will be too late for those who have spent a lifetime ignoring Him when He returns to claim His earthly kingdom by force. Yes, that gentle God the world only sees as a loving, peaceful Creator is coming in a whirlwind of anger and fury! **Woe unto the wicked and Christ rejecting sinners and** all the Devil's minions in that day!

God Is A Trinity

God is a tripartite being. He has three parts. Although He is **one** God, He has **three** distinct personalities: God the Father, God the Son and God the Holy Spirit. The Bible has this to say on the subject: *"For there are three that bear record in heaven, the Father, the Word, and the Holy Ghost: and these three are one."* (I John 5:7)

The scripture is very plain here about the three parts of God since John 1:1-14 identifies Who the **Word** is. The **Word** is Jesus!

Here is the breakdown of God's three part nature:
1) God the Father..................the Soul
2) God the Son.........the Body (Jesus)
3) God the Holy Ghost........the Spirit.

So, we see that the one true God is made up of three parts and has a tripartite nature. Therefore, since man was made in the image of God according to scripture, he, too, is a trinity having a body, a soul and a spirit! *"And God said, Let us make man in our image, after our likeness:... So God created man in his own image, in the image of God created he him: male and female created he them."* (Gen. 1:26-27)

"And the Word was made flesh and dwelt among us...." John 1:14

There we see that man was created with three parts like God. The Apostle Paul understood and accepted this three part man, as

35

evidenced in his letter to the Thessalonians: *"And the very God of peace sanctify you wholly; and I pray God your whole <u>spirit</u> and <u>soul</u> and <u>body</u> be preserved blameless unto the coming of our Lord Jesus Christ."* (I Thess. 5:23)

A God Of Love

Our God is a loving, merciful and kind hearted - God. Love is synonymous with God. In fact, God **is** Love. *"He that loveth not knoweth not God; for <u>God is love.</u> [9] In this was manifested the love of God toward us, because that God sent his only begotten Son into the world, that we might live through him."* (I John 4:8-9)

The Bible is full of verses where God states His love for mankind, as well as verses showing that great love through His actions toward us. There can be no greater love than to give one's life for that of another and that is exactly what God did for us. He left Heaven and came down to earth in human form to die for the sins of the world so that we may live. *"This is my commandment, That ye love one another, as I have loved you. [13] Greater love hath no man than this, that a man lay down his life for his friends."* (John 15:12-13) And, *"For God so loved the world, that he gave his only begotten Son, that whosoever believeth in him should not perish, but have everlasting life."* (John 3:16)

"Greater love hath no man than this, that a man lay down his life for his friends." (John 15:13)

God created man so that He may love and be loved in return. He even loved us before we were saved. *"But God, who is rich in mercy, for his great love*

36

wherewith he loved us, [5]Even when we were dead in sins, hath quickened us together with Christ, (by grace ye are saved;)" (Eph. 2:4-5)

God The Savior

From man's standpoint, outside of His holiness, God's grace is the most important attribute. Because of the grace of God, man was given as a free gift, a way to redeem himself from his sinful nature. (Eph 2:8, Rom 5:12) Although God Himself is holy and righteous, He is also a forgiving God who does not want us to die in our sins and face a burning Hell for all eternity. (II Pet. 3:9, Rom. 6:23)

Because He loved us, He was willing to leave Heaven, a perfect and righteous place, and come down to a wicked and sinful earth, to suffer, bleed and die for our sins. Thank God that He loved us enough to die for us and give us a chance to be redeemed! *"But God commendeth his love toward us, in that, while we were yet sinners, Christ died for us. [9] Much more then, being now justified by his blood, we shall be saved from wrath through him."* (Rom.5:8-9)

Have you ever considered how great His love for you really was? Few have. However, we have all seen His suffering redundantly characterized in both movies and books by the blood-letting and marring of His flesh being ripped to shreds by the whip and the inhumane beating He received. The Bible says, He was *"....marred more than any man.."* (Isa. 52:14) and our sympathy has always focused on the physical pain He endured for us.

But as immense and colossal as that pain and suffering was,

it pales in comparison to the mental and emotional trauma experienced when the sins of the world fell full force on a holy and righteous God! This encompasses all the sins from the beginning of time to the end of sin at the White Throne Judgment. Such a traumatic event that God the Father even momentarily turned away, prompting Jesus to cry, *"my God, my god, why hast thou forsaken me?"* (Matt. 27:46)

How can we know or even imagine the magnitude of His love for us that prompted Him to leave the glories of Heaven and come to earth to be made sin for us that we may live and walk in His Holy Light? *"For he hath made him to be sin for us, who knew no sin; that we might be made the righteousness of God in him."* (II Cor. 5:21)

His love should be enough to make everyone not only desire to be saved, but also desire to love and serve Jesus faithfully. Obviously, He wants us all to be saved. *"The Lord is not slack concerning his promise, as some men count slackness; but is longsuffering to us-ward, not willing that any should perish, but that all should come to repentance."* (II Pet. 3:9)

"For this is good and acceptable in the sight of God our Savior; [4] Who will have all men to be saved, and to come unto the knowledge of the truth." (1 Tim. 2:3-4) *"Behold, the eye of the Lord is upon them that fear him, upon them that hope in his mercy; [19] To deliver their soul from death, and to keep them alive in famine."* (Ps. 33:18-19)

Hopefully, you can claim the next verse for your own life. *"Lead me in thy truth, and teach me: for thou art the God of my salvation; on thee do I wait all the day."* (Ps. 25:5)   The same Savior who loved us so much (John 3:16) will one day become a God of wrath for those who reject His free gift of salvation.

God is Omnipotent

In other words, God is all powerful. His power and authority over all things is unlimited. He has the power to speak things into existence. God said *"let there be light:"* and there was light. He said *"let there be a firmament..,"* and there was a firmament. He said *"let the dry land appear ..,"* and it appeared. He said *"let there be light in the firmament of heaven,"* (Gen. 1) and it was so. The whole universe was created with the spoken word. *"For he spake, and it was done; he commanded, and it stood fast."* (Ps. 33:9)

I once heard a government worker say, *"We've done so much, for so long, with so little, that now we can do anything with nothing!"* Well, obviously that was an exaggeration for man, but God can truly create without anything with which to work or begin! There is only one thing God cannot do. He cannot sin. That would be against His holy and righteous nature.

There is nothing outside of or beyond God's power. He can give life or take life away, and then bring it back again. He can make the poor rich or the rich poor. He speaks, and it happens, He wills and it takes place. There is none that has power over Him!

"The Lord killeth, and maketh alive: he bringeth down to the grave, and bringeth up. [7] The Lord maketh poor, and maketh rich: he bringeth low, and lifteth up. [8] He raiseth up the poor out of the dust, and lifteth up the beggar from the dunghill, to

set them among princes, and to make them inherit the throne of glory: for the pillars of the earth are the Lord's, and he hath set the world upon them." (I Sam. 2:6-8)

".......neither is there any that can deliver out of my hand." (Deut. 32:39) *"Thine, O Lord, is the greatness, and the power, and the glory, and the victory, and the majesty: for all that is in the heaven and in the earth is thine; thine is the kingdom, O Lord, and thou art exalted as head above all. [12] Both riches and honour come of thee, and thou reignest over all; and in thine hand is power and might; and in thine hand it is to make great, and to give strength unto all. [13]Now therefore, our God, we thank thee, and praise thy glorious name."* (I Chr. 29:11-13)

God's power and authority extends to every person, every place and every thing in the universe. His power and abilities are beyond the understanding or even the imagination of man.

God is Omniscient

God is all knowing. He knows everything about you! Your every word, your every thought! Scary, isn't it? His understanding is without end. *".....There is no searching of His understanding."* (Isa. 40:26) Your very thoughts are an open book to Him who is all knowing and all seeing! *"Then Job answered the Lord, and said, [2] I know that thou canst do every thing, and that no thought can be withholden from thee."* (Job 42:1-2)

And, *"Neither is there any creature that is not manifest in his sight: but all things are naked and opened unto the eyes of him with whom we have to do."* (Heb. 4:13)

There are no secrets before Him. *"....for there is nothing covered, that shall not be revealed; and hid, that shall not be known."* (Matt. 10:26) He sees it all! *"For the eyes of the Lord run to and fro throughout the whole earth, to shew himself strong in the behalf of them whose heart is perfect toward him."* (II Chr. 16:9)

Moreover, God has foreseen every possible thought and intent of the heart of man. He has dealt with it in the Bible which was written thousands of years before you even had the thought or intent in your heart!   *"For the word of God is quick, and powerful, and sharper than any twoedged sword, piercing even to the dividing asunder of soul and spirit, and of the joints and marrow, and is a discerner of the thoughts and intents of the heart."* (Heb 4:12) He even has the hairs on every person's head numbered! *"But the very hairs of your head are all numbered."* (Matt. 10:30)

There is nowhere to hide from or to escape from an omniscient God. So why not receive Him, love Him, obey Him, serve and fellowship with Him?

God Is Omnipresent

God is everywhere! There is no place in the universe you could be that He would not be present. You can't get away from Him because He is in every place at the same time. Our mind simply cannot comprehend the vastness of God and His ability to be omnipresent, omniscient and omnipotent. As for His being omnipresent, David put it well in Ps. 139:7-10. *"Whither shall I go from thy spirit? or whither shall I flee from thy presence? [8] If I ascend up into heaven, thou art there: if I make my bed in*

41

hell, behold, thou art there. [9] If I take the wings of the morning, and dwell in the uttermost parts of the sea; [10] Even there shall thy hand lead me, and thy right hand shall hold me."

There are no secret places where one can hide from God. He is always here. *"Am I a God at hand, saith the Lord, and not a God afar off? [24] Can any hide himself in secret places that I shall not see him? saith the Lord. Do not I fill heaven and earth? saith the Lord."* (Jer. 23:23-24) You cannot even hide in your dreams because the Lord is there also. God spoke to Jacob as he slept. *"And Jacob awaked out of his sleep, and he said, Surely the Lord is in this place; and I knew it not."* (Gen. 28:16)

This is why it is fruitless to run from God and His will for our life. There is no escape; there is no way to overcome or to win against a holy and all powerful God. For the Christian, there is no peace, contentment, or happiness outside of living and walking in the Spirit with Him. You can't beat Him, so join Him. Then you will be happier and reap the rewards and fruits of the Spirit in Christ.

A God Of Wrath

Few people think of God as an angry God or a God of wrath. However, we must understand that although He is a loving God, He is perfectly balanced, and so being, is also a God of tremendous wrath. God is Holy and righteous and hates sin; therefore, His wrath is kindled by sin and wickedness. *"God judgeth the righteous, and God is angry with the wicked every day."* (Ps. 7:11)

The fear of the Lord is the beginning of wisdom: ...Ps. 111:10

The average person pictures God as

42

some great big lovable Santa Claus and this is definitely not the picture our Bible paints. ***"The Lord is a man of war: the Lord is his name."*** (Ex.15:3) That verse would drive the anti-war crowd nuts, but they would really crash and burn on this next one:

"I have trodden the winepress alone; and of the people there was none with me: for I will tread them in mine anger, and trample them in my fury; and their blood shall be sprinkled upon my garments, and I will stain all my raiment. [4] For the day of vengeance is in mine heart, and the year of my redeemed is come." (Isa. 63:3-4) Or this one.....

"And I saw heaven opened, and behold a white horse; and he that sat upon him was called Faithful and True, and in righteousness he doth judge and make war. [12] His eyes were as a flame of fire, and on his head were many crowns; and he had a name written, that no man knew, but he himself. [13] And he was clothed with a vesture dipped in blood: and his name is called The Word of God. [14] And the armies which were in heaven followed him upon white horses, clothed in fine linen, white and clean. [15] And out of his mouth goeth a sharp sword, that with it he should smite the nations: and he shall rule them with a rod of iron: and he treadeth the winepress of the fierceness and wrath of Almighty God. [16] And he hath on his vesture and on his thigh a name written, KING OF KINGS, AND LORD OF LORDS. [17] And I saw an angel standing in the sun; and he cried with a loud voice, saying to all the fowls that fly in the midst of heaven, Come and gather yourselves together unto the supper of the great God; [18] That ye may eat the flesh of kings, and the flesh of captains, and the flesh of mighty men, and the flesh of horses, and of them that sit on

them, and the flesh of all men, both free and bond, both small and great. " (Rev. 19:11-18)

My, my, but isn't that a different God than what most people have in mind! By this time (Rev. 19:11-18) it's too late and many will be crying out for death rather than face an angry God.. *"And the kings of the earth, and the great men, and the rich men, and the chief captains, and the mighty men, and every bondman, and every free man, hid themselves in the dens and in the rocks of the mountains; [16] And said to the mountains and rocks, Fall on us, and hide us from the face of him that sitteth on the throne, and from the wrath of the Lamb: [17] For the great day of his wrath is come; and who shall be able to stand?"* (Rev. 6:15-17)

A Jealous God

Our God is a jealous God. He will not allow the worship of other gods to go unpunished. *"Thou shalt not bow down thyself to them, nor serve them: for I the Lord thy God am a jealous God, visiting the iniquity of the fathers upon the children unto the third and fourth generation of them that hate me;"* (Ex. 20:5) *"God is jealous, and the Lord revengeth; the Lord revengeth, and is furious; the Lord will take vengeance on his adversaries, and he reserveth wrath for his enemies.* (Nah. 1:2)

He is so jealous the scripture even gives "Jealous" as one of His names. *"For thou shalt worship no other god: for the Lord, whose name is Jealous, is a jealous God:"* (Ex. 34:14) It doesn't take many of these verses for one to get the picture that He will not put up with you putting anything ahead of Him! *"Woe to the rebellious children, saith the Lord, that take counsel, but not of me; and that cover with a covering, but not of my spirit,*

that they may add sin to sin:" (Isa. 30:1)

The child of God should be very careful not to put anything or anyone ahead of God in their heart. He may very well take away that thing you count more worthy of your love and attention than Him. He wants to be number one in our life, ahead of family, friends, job, hobbies, etc. He wants your heart and soul. When you really surrender to Him, your happiness and reward will be great.

God's Names

God has many names, some of which are also used in reference to the Lord Jesus Christ. Some of the most common are: "Everlasting Father," "Jehovah" or "Lord," "Mighty God," "Alpha and Omega," "Lord of Lords" and many, many more commonly used names. We will also list some of the less common names and their meaning. We will first give the Hebrew name and then the interpretation in English.

1. **"Elohim"** = "One who is mighty" or "The Lord who creates."
2. **"Elelyon"** = "The One who is supreme" or "the Lord who owns."
3. **"Adonai"** = "The Lord our Master" or "The one who is ruling."
4. **"El olam"** = "The One who reveals Himself" or "The One who is mysterious."
5. **"Jehovah jireh"** = "The Lord who provides."
6. **"Jehovah nissi"** = "The Lord our Banner."
7. **"Jehovah rapha"** = "The One who heals."
8. **"El Shaddai"** = "The all sufficient One."
9. **"Jehovah shalom"** = "The Lord our Peace."

10. **"Jehovah sabaoth "** = "The Lord of Hosts."
11. **"Jehovah tsidkenu"** = "The Lord of our Righteousness."
12. **"Jehovah shammah"** = "The One present" or 'The One close by."
13. **"Jehovah elyon"** = "The One who is blessing" or 'The Lord our Blesser."
14. **"Jehovah raah"** = "The Lord our Shepherd."

In conclusion, we have given only a few of the characteristics of God. There are many more such as: His *chastisement, wisdom, faithfulness, fatherhood, goodness, grace, longsuffering, mercy* etc. However, you should have a better understanding of God than you did prior to this chapter. There is much more to be found in the Bible on this subject. In fact you could write a whole book on the characteristics and the nature of God. He is a mighty God, an awesome God. Worship Him!!

So, now that the reader has been introduced to God's desire for fellowship, the condition of today's Church and the nature of God, it is reasonable to assume that you have already evaluated your own spiritual condition with respect to this matter of fellowship.

Chances are, you believe you already are engaged in this daily fellowship and presently enjoy the treasures that abound in Christ. Or maybe you feel you just have some measure of it with room for improvement. Then again, you may suddenly realize you don't have it at all. Whichever group you fall into (if you desire a sustaining fellowship with Him) there are pitfalls of which you need to be aware of and avoid in the Christian life.

Be forewarned. This is not a "feel good" book, but rather a practical guide to help you achieve your goal. So, view the next several chapters as a foundation. In these chapters you will see some things you need to put into practice and some you need to avoid in pursuit of your goal (of a sustained fellowship) as we introduce you to the most common influences that qualify as "fellowship killers."

Chapter 4

Beware The Fellowship Killer #1

"Study to shew thyself approved unto God, a workman that needeth not to be ashamed, rightly dividing the word of truth." II Tim. 2:15

As every "Spirit filled" Christian knows, there are many pitfalls in the world today just waiting to trip up anyone who dares to try to *"walk in the light"* and to be close to the Lord Jesus Christ. Our society is a literal mine field for the child of God who must circumnavigate disaster daily as he journeys through a lost and sinful world. The next few chapters are to highlight some of the more common enemies of the Christian's spiritual walk and to offer some guidelines on what to avoid.

False Doctrine

The purpose of this book is to impress on the Christian that the most important thing in his or her life is fellowship with the Lord Jesus Christ and to offer suggestions on how to achieve that goal. However, if you are saved and are not practicing sound doctrine there can be little real "fellowship" because you are disobedient and out of the "will of God." So, in such a case the most important thing is to get the doctrine correct and restore fellowship. Of course, if you are unsaved, then false doctrine can keep you from being saved. Therefore, sound doctrine is not only important, it is critical.

As we have explained in earlier lessons, sound doctrine, as it relates to the Christian, means the <u>correct</u> teaching on fundamentals of the faith. Hence, the phrase, "Christian doctrine." Important doctrines of the Christian faith would include subjects such as: the way to salvation, the trinity of God, the deity of Christ, eternal security of the believer, teachings on Heaven and Hell, how we should live as Christians, separation from unbelievers, prayer and forgiveness, to name a few. These studies and much more can be found in detail in the *Bread Of Life Bible Believers Fundamental Bible Study Course* (2002) by the writer.

Why Sound Doctrine Is Important

Christian doctrine is important because it comes from God Himself. *"Jesus answered them, and said, My doctrine is not mine, but his that sent me."* (John 7:16) God counts it important because He wants us all to be saved (II Pet. 3:9). If you don't

> *My doctrine is not mine, but his that sent me. 17 If any man will do his will, he shall know of the doctrine, whether it be of God, or whether I speak of myself.* John 7:16-17

have the proper doctrinal teaching on salvation, you may believe you are saved, but in reality you are lost and on your way to Hell!

Just because you believe with all your heart that something is right <u>does not</u> make it right and acceptable to God. The Bible warns us about trusting our feelings. *"There is a way which seemeth right unto a man, but*

49

the end thereof are the ways of death. " (Prov.14:12)

The Gospel is the plan of salvation. That is why it is so important. The one *true* Gospel is the death, burial and resurrection of Jesus Christ. (I Cor. 15:1-4) He died for the sins of the world, He was buried and rose from the dead, defeating

> But though we, or an angel from heaven, preach any other gospel unto you than that which we have preached unto you, let him be accursed. Gal. 1:8

death and Hell for you and me. The only way you can get to Heaven is to trust His sacrifice and resurrection as a full and complete payment for your sins and through prayer, ask for forgiveness and receive HIM as your Savior. (Rom. 10:9-10)

It is not the Gospel plus something your church added from tradition, or something else they said you had to do in addition to believe. It is the Gospel plus nothing! Actually, it's this simple; If you want to go to Heaven, trust Jesus Christ and Him alone. If you want to go to Hell, trust something else, someone else or Jesus plus something more! That's not trying to be mean, or to criticize anyone's religion; it's simply the word of God. (Gal. 1:8)

Basically it comes down to this: a person is either a **Bible believer**, accepting scripture for scripture in the correct context, or a **Bible rejecter**. Bible rejecters cite verses out of context, add to, take away or use fragmented verses to wrest the scripture and make it teach what they desire.

This fosters many false teachings and heresies, not all of which involve salvation, but are still deadly to the Christian's spiritual growth and fellowship with God. Later in the book we will show the reader how to sort out these doctrines and determine which ones are directed to the child of God in the "Church Age" in which we live.

So, we find ourselves at a point in time where teaching the Bible and sound doctrine is a stranger in most churches although the charge to do so is very clear in II Tim 4:2-4. Notice the scripture also described a coming apostasy in the church (which has now arrived). *Preach the word; be instant in season, out of season; reprove, rebuke, exhort with all longsuffering and doctrine. [3] For the time will come when they will not endure sound doctrine; but after their own lusts shall they heap to themselves teachers, having itching ears; [4] And they shall turn away their ears from the truth, and shall be turned unto fables.*

And again in I Tim. 4:1: *Now the Spirit speaketh expressly, that in the latter times some shall depart from the faith, giving heed to seducing spirits, and doctrines of devils; [2] Speaking lies in hypocrisy; having their conscience seared with a hot iron;* God forgive us for allowing what most of today's churches have become!

Many pastors shy away from doctrinal issues because they say it divides. Well, duh! That's what God intended it to do, so as to separate the truth from a lie. ie: the true Gospel (I Cor 15:1-4) from one under a curse (Gal. 1:8), light from darkness, etc. The truth is, many pastors don't know enough Bible to deal with doctrinal matters scripturally so they choose to avoid any controversy to cover for their own scriptural ignorance.

51

The Apostle Paul, who God sent to bring us the New Testament covenant (Acts 9:15) addressed this issue in no uncertain terms when he warned Timothy about false doctrine in I Tim. 4:1. *"Now the Spirit speaketh expressly, that in the latter times some shall depart from the faith, giving heed to seducing spirits, and doctrines of devils;"*

He also had some very plain and emphatic words in his letter to the Galatians, who apparently were straying from sound doctrine and the true Gospel. *"I marvel that ye are so soon removed from him that called you into the grace of Christ unto another gospel: [7] Which is not another; but there be some that trouble you, and would pervert the gospel of Christ. [8] But though we, or an angel from heaven, preach any other gospel unto you than that which we have preached unto you, let him be accursed. [9] As we said before, so say I now again, If any man preach any other gospel unto you than that ye have received, let him be accursed."* (Gal. 1:6-9) There it is, plain and simple!

> *For my thoughts are not your thoughts, neither are your ways my ways, saith the Lord. [9] For as the heavens are higher than the earth, so are my ways higher than your ways, and my thoughts than your thoughts.* Isa. 55:8-9

Notice that Paul considered it so important that he repeated himself in the next verse so they wouldn't miss the gravity of what he said. Notice also, that anyone teaching a false Gospel (false doctrine) is under a curse!!

Notice again that the word of God is not concerned about being politically correct or about being tolerant! God is a very <u>intolerant</u> being and couldn't care less about good intentions, or if people get their feelings hurt. He is interested in them getting the truth about His Son Jesus Christ so they can escape a burning Hell! So if you thought I was a bit harsh earlier, it is because souls are at stake!

That is why Paul's statement (as given by God) is one of the most intolerant statements in the Bible. And incidently, there are many such like statements. God is not interested in what any God denying, Bible rejecting non-believer thinks about what is right or wrong, good or bad, politically correct or incorrect. Their wisdom is foolishness to Him, (I Cor. 1:19, 2:5, 3:19) and He will laugh when their destruction comes! (Prov. 1:25-28) So, "study" and get it right while there is time! (II Tim. 2:15)

There are many other scripture references concerning this subject that the student should study. A few of those are:

* We are admonished to speak with sound doctrine in Tit. 2:1. ***"But speak thou the things which become sound doctrine:"***

* We are not to steal, (purloining) but to show good fidelity. ***"Not purloining, but shewing all good fidelity; that they may adorn the doctrine of God our Savior in all things."*** (Tit. 2:10)

* Paul also warned that people will not always endure sound doctrine. ***"Preach the word; be instant in season, out of season; reprove, rebuke, exhort with all longsuffering and doctrine. [3] For the time will come when they will not endure sound doctrine; but after their own lusts shall they heap to themselves*** *teachers, having itching ears;"* (II Tim. 4:2-3)

* Elders are counted worthy of double honor if they labor in the word and doctrine in I Tim 5:17.

* Christians should not chase every new or different doctrine that comes along, but rather learn to rightly divide the word. *"That we henceforth be no more children, tossed to and fro, and carried about with every wind of doctrine, by the sleight of men, and cunning craftiiness, whereby they lie in wait to deceive;"* (Eph. 4:14)

What Is The Cause Of False Doctrine?

Sound doctrine is "rightly dividing" the word of God, nothing more, nothing less. We are commanded to study so we can do just that! *"Study to shew thyself approved unto God, a workman that needeth not to be ashamed, rightly dividing the word of truth."* (II Tim. 2:15)

It is worth noting that the word **"study"** is not in the new Bibles. Who do you think doesn't want you to study your Bible? God or the

> *"..Satan cometh immediately, and taketh away the word..."*
> Mark 4:15

Devil? As for false doctrine, the problem is most people don't study on their own and are not <u>taught</u> how to rightly divide the Word in their church. Often this is because their pastor was never taught how himself.

This is the reason we have so many different denominations and why some are teaching a false Gospel along with other false doctrines. The cause of this, and the result of not "rightly dividing" the word is twofold:

1) False doctrines are always based on a few verses that are added to, taken away from, or taken out of context. Coupled with ignoring the many verses in the proper context that <u>prove the false teaching wrong</u>. So, verses are taken out of context to make the Bible <u>teach what people want it to</u>, while they ignore what it <u>said</u> in the context in which it was written. This is done largely through ignorance and lack of

> *"...for ye have perverted the words of the living God,...."* Jer. 23:36

serious Bible study. You can make the Bible "teach" almost anything with this approach.

2) People take verses that apply to saints in another age (such as the Old Testament times, the Tribulation, or the Millennium) and try to place them doctrinally in this present Church Age. This creates confusion because it makes the Bible appear to contradict itself, when we know it doesn't.

So, the <u>heresies taught in our Church Age are usually proper doctrine for another Age</u> such as the Old Testament Age (under the Law), the Tribulation or Millennium. Consequently, if you understand that the false doctrine taught today was a truth in another time, you can put many confusing verses in their proper context. The key is to learn how to find the proper context so you can rightly divide for yourself.

In so doing, you will be able to discern the Biblical truth of controversial teachings such as: water baptism necessary for salvation in the Church Age, or "Sabbath Day" worship, or <u>any</u> works being necessary for salvation in the Church Age, and the issue of eternal security of the Church Age believer.

All these examples are explained in detail and backed up with Scripture in the writers previous work, "Bible Believer's Fundamental Bible Study Course." These are too long to repeat here. However, the reader may want to acquire that work and examine some examples of rightly dividing. Henceforth, we are about to briefly show you how to do it yourself.

Remember! Let the Bible be your "final authority," not people! The Bible means what it says, and says what it means in the context in which it is written. So, what it <u>says</u> is important, not what someone can make it teach by wresting the scriptures.

It is really amazing how some will argue all day long about some Bible teaching they have never really studied themselves! Rather, they rely on what some religious friend or preacher says simply because they like the person and want to believe them. This is the "blind leading the blind" and <u>could earn both an eternal home in the Lake of Fire</u>.

> *Search the scriptures; for in them ye think ye have eternal life: and they are they which testify of me.* John 5:39

Rightly Dividing
Scripture has three applications, and it is important to determine

if a certain verse, or verses, actually has "doctrinal" application to you in the "Church Age" dispensation in which we presently live. The three applications of scripture are as follows:

1) Historical: Meaning either past, present or future. **2) Spiritual:** Spiritual or practical in everyday life. **3) Doctrinal:** God's instruction to those in a particular age or dispensation. It is the teaching on things such as salvation, eternal security of the believer and how people of a particular age should live to please God. <u>Some doctrines change in different ages under different covenants</u>. This is confusing to those who fail to rightly divide.

Naturally, all scripture applies to us historically and spiritually. However, not all scripture applies to us now in the Church Age **doctrinally** as God changes some doctrinal things from one age to another. Therefore, the next approach in helping you rightly divide the word is to ask the following questions when you analyze a particular portion of scripture:

1) Who is this particular book, chapter or verse addressing? Is it a nation, an individual or a certain group of people? Old Testament Jew under the Law, Church Age Saint, Tribulation or Millennial Saint?

2) When is this period of time? Is it before or after the Resurrection of Christ, during the Tribulation or Millennium? If it is before the resurrection or after the Rapture, it is not a Church Age application and would **not** apply to Christians *doctrinally*.

3) What is the context (main subject) of the chapter or verse, and in what dispensation does that place it? A good example is

Matthew 24. Some try to put verse 13 in the Church Age, but the whole chapter is a Tribulation context and does not apply doctrinally to Christian Saints.

Asking these questions will help you determine if a verse applies to you <u>doctrinally</u> in the Church Age or if it belongs in some other dispensation. For example, is it addressing people in the past or people in the future after the Church Age? A helpful rule to remember is that <u>all</u> the Pauline epistles (Romans to Philemon) apply to the Church Age Christian **doctrinally**.

Although some doctrines addressed in other New Testament books may also have application doctrinally in this age, many don't and must be examined in light of the method described above. The books of the Bible from which most modern heresies are extracted are: Acts, Matthew and Hebrews. You really need to be careful trying to apply doctrines from these books to the Church Age. Just remember, <u>all</u> of the Bible applies to us **spiritually** and **historically**, but not **doctrinally**. If we rightly dividing the word, the Bible will not contradict itself.

You have been given the tools to rightly divide the word. Put them to good use and be sure the doctrine, on which you stand, is sound and pleasing to God.

```
══════════
══════════
```

Chapter 5

```
══════════
══════════
```

Beware The Fellowship Killer #2

*"Love not the world, neither the things that are in the
world. If any man love the world, the love of the Father is
not in him."* I John 2:15

Worldliness

Every Christian is called to be a Christian soldier (II Tim. 2:3)
and every good soldier should make it a point to know his enemy
well. The Christian has many enemies, but the three (3) major
ones are the world, the flesh and the devil. <u>If you are to be a
working, God pleasing, Spirit filled Christian</u>, you need a good
general knowledge of these enemies and the dangers they present,
along with the methods they use to attack your Christian life and
testimony.

The reader may well be shocked as we define, expose, and
identify these enemies and their tactics. While you may disagree
with some of the comments, remember, that the Bible should be
your final authority in all matters of faith and practice applying
verses in the proper context. The Scripture has much to say about
the "world" and the opinions of men.

When we speak of the "world," we are <u>not</u> talking about the earth, and the untold beauty of it's mountains, seas, forests, and natural wonders. But rather, we are talking about the wicked, ungodly, God denying, Christ rejecting, humanistic world system around us. This includes: all places, things, and activities of the world that separate us from, and oppose all light from the Living God.

Following are some examples of worldly things of which a Christian should beware and how the world, in general, is blatantly contrary to a holy and righteous God.

While you may wonder why we are going into some of this, rest assured that the Spirit filled, Bible believing Christian needs to be acutely aware of his surroundings. Since it is impractical to try and list everything, we will just mention some of the major things you need to be aware of, avoid, and separate yourself from, as you pursue fellowship with Him.

1. Liberalism and secular humanism: The largest problem in our society today and the root of it's condition is that people **do not fear God**. This attitude is brought on by a multitude of problems in our present society.

> *The fear of God is the beginning of wisdom:* Prov. 9:10

However, at the top of the list you will find **liberalism** and **secular humanism firmly entrenched in our schools and society** working to remove God from the American way of life!

These are not just some moralistic, or political view points, but rather should be considered a <u>new and dangerous religion</u>. Although there are "mild" liberals that are not yet as extreme "left

60

wing" as the secular humanists, <u>they all reject God and His Word</u>. We used to laugh at these people early on, little realizing the impact their relentless assault would have on the Christian values once embedded in our society.

The word "**liberal**" means more than just being broad minded. It means not restricted, or **not limited to the literal interpretation** of the Bible, according to Webster's dictionary. It means "reform" in religion to match a progressive society. **In other words, the liberal will change God's rules to match his own modern day beliefs and purposes**.

Woe unto them that reject the Light!

The word "**secular**" simply means not religious, not bound to any recognized church or religion (they have their own). The word "**humanism**" reflects a philosophy centered on man himself, his condition, accomplishments, goals, and so-forth. Here are some revealing points:

* Humanists are, by and large, **atheists**, although some are deists who profess some "form of God," but still reject the Bible as God's word. They will, however, often quote the Bible out of context to prove their own view. But they refuse to be limited to God's rules, but rather rationalize their own morals based on <u>emotion</u> and their own warped logic. They believe man can work out his own problems and will eventually progress to perfection by himself. In general, they are concerned with the material things of this life and are not concerned with God or the souls of men.

* More often than not, they are **socialists politically,** and don't believe man has enough sense to take care of himself. Consequently, he needs <u>big government to watch over and take care of him</u>. Simply put, they favor a communist system over capitalism. Communism is a two class system, the rich leaders and the poor. There is no middle class in the communist system as presently exists (although it is fast disappearing) in America.

Big government loves to have numerous and diverse social programs and services. The people then become dependent on this support and subsequently are easily controlled. The capitalistic system (as we know it) along with the freedom and liberty it promotes, is gone and the common people are ruled by the police state. Therefore, the people in a socialist society are little more than slaves to their rulers. This is the agenda of the liberal, socialist political system as they strive to destroy the America we know. It matters not one bit to these that this system has failed in countries all over the world.

* Most are evolutionists that reject the Bible's account of God and creation. They trust science rather than God to bring man to his perfection through the evolution of knowledge.

* The liberal humanist is an **extreme environmentalist**. While it's good to protect and enhance our

> *There is a way which seemeth right unto a man, but the end thereof are the ways of death.* Prov. 14:12

environment and wildlife, it is a sin to worship the "creation" instead of the "creator!" *"Who changed the truth of God into a lie, and worshipped and served the creature more than the*

Creator, who is blessed for ever. Amen." (Rom. 1:25)

God said they are liars! For example, they are more concerned about saving the trees or the endangered woodpeckers, whales, manatees and so forth, than they are about the unborn human babies being murdered every day by abortion. It is not uncommon to see a liberal's vehicle with a "pro-choice" bumper sticker on one side and a "save the manatee" on the other side. Kill the babies, but save the animals and trees. Unbelievable!

This is what happens when people reject God and His written word which gives us laws and precepts by which to live. This is a society headed for destruction unless it turns back to God. The liberals ignore God and believe anything is alright if the end result is for the "common good," <u>as they see it.</u> It doesn't matter if it is against God's law or man's law. In other words the "end justifies the means." An example of this occurred several years ago when the anti-hunters were shooting at deer hunters in south Florida as they sat in their deer stands. Save the deer, murder the hunter! Insane!

* This new religion (without God) has infiltrated our public education system and is brainwashing our children. We have allowed them to force prayer and even the Bible out of our schools. The result is an inept education system which is in shambles. We have Bible verses and the Ten Commandments all over our federal buildings in Washington and even on the Liberty Bell. We have "in God we trust" on our money, yet all these things that were alright for two hundred (200) years are suddenly unacceptable to a few.

What's worse, is that this secularism has all but taken over our higher court system where judges are rewriting the Constitution with opinions and verdicts contrary to that great document upon which our country was founded.

Patrick Henry, a patriot and founding father of our country said, *"it cannot be emphasized too strongly or too often that this great nation was founded not by religionists but by Christians, not on religions but on the Gospel of Jesus Christ."* So why are we allowing a few misguided individuals to remove God from the American way of life?

If left unchecked, these people will create a secular (Godless) society. They are ruthless, and you can be assured they will try to destroy anything or anyone in the way of their goal. This new religion is more than just a passing trend and is already well on the way to destroying America. This destruction is being done primarily by eliminating America's Christian ties and destroying

> **The wicked shall be turned into hell, and all the nations that forget God.** Ps. 9:17

our capitalistic system. These are the very attributes which have made America the richest and strongest country the world has ever known.

This is a religion that promotes big socialistic government which rules the people rather than serving them. It is an anti- God, anti-Christ, anti-freedom, anti-middle class, anti-marriage, anti-family, anti-gun, anti-hunting, pro abortion monstrosity that has rejected the light of the word of God. If God's people in America don't wake up (and soon) it will be too late! The Christian needs to realize that we are in a serious battle (Eph. 6). We need to speak out and fight against the tenants of this new ungodly religion at every opportunity, with prayer and with the Sword of the Spirit.

* Beware of worldliness that enters through your eyes and ears. The eyes and ears are doorways to the soul. What Christians allow to <u>enter the eyes and ears</u> can be a great help or a tremendous hindrance to their spiritual growth. For example, the type of music to which you listen is extremely important. The Devil has used music for years to draw people away from God.

Rock music is the worst, most of it being absolutely demonic. And remember, there is

> *The light of the body is the eye: therefore when thine eye is single, thy whole body also is full of light; but when thine eye is evil, thy body also is full of darkness. 35 Take heed therefore, that the light which is in thee be not darkness.* Luke 11:34-35

no such thing as Christian rock! I realize some may not agree with that assessment, but the proof is already in; the die is cast, and the Church (body of Christ) as a whole is in apostasy (Rev. 3:14-17).

The devil's message through this media is often subliminal (not noticeable to the conscious mind) and enters the sub-conscious mind, thereby doing the damage without your being aware. But, it's not just the music with which you need to be cautious. Be careful of anything you listen to and allow to enter your mind! Feed the mind with spiritual and godly material, not the junk of unsaved people and the world. They worship the wrong gods!

What you **"see"** and those things that enter in through the eyes are also extremely important in keeping your "temple" clean. Remember, the body is the temple of the indwelling Holy Spirit for all that are saved. *"What? know ye not that your body is the temple of the Holy Ghost which is in you, which ye have of God, and ye are not your own? [20] For ye are bought with a price: therefore glorify God in your body, and in your spirit, which are God's."* (I Cor. 6:19-20)

So, if you are to keep your temple clean and in order, you must be very careful about television and movies and the internet. Without a doubt, these are the greatest sources of spiritual pollution in America today. Granted, some movies can be good entertainment or great educational tools with proper content. However, the Christian must be very careful of the programs they watch and allow their children to watch.

The mind is affected by what goes in through the eyes and, unfortunately, there is plenty of trash around today. **Little could hinder your fellowship with God more than what you see**. The TV, video and internet media today are primary sources for this garbage. The dominant subject matter is centered around sex and violence. They promote pornography, adultery, sexual perversion, fornication, sex outside of marriage, foul language, worshipping of the body, the use of drugs, alcohol, violence and murder. **It is "spiritual suicide" to let this trash enter your mind through your eyes or by any other means when possible to avoid it.**

It is not only bad for adults, but also, the consequences of children viewing this trash is tragic. Children as young as nine or ten years old are having sex, stealing and even murdering their school mates, brothers, sisters, and parents. Many later admit they learned how to do this on TV. The adult Christian must realize that such programing is produced by unregenerated mankind (lost people) for the purpose of making money and is extremely harmful to your relationship with God. **Don't let it be your personal downfall and come between you and your spiritual fellowship and walk with the Lord!**

* Be careful with written material as well. Naturally, there are numerous other ways you can allow the wrong influences to enter through the eyes. There is as much (or more) **written material** that is ungodly as there is in the visual media. However, the average person does not read as much as they did before the TV came along. Nevertheless, you must be just as careful of the written garbage as the visual kind. Whether you see it, hear it or read it, the subject remains in your sub-conscious mind and can return to cause problems later. Everyone has sinful images from the past that pop up occasionally, but if you don't put them there in the first place, then you don't have to worry about them coming back!

* Your mouth is also a doorway for worldly things such as alcohol, drugs, unhealthy foods, and more to enter and harm your body. Remember, the body is the temple of the Holy Spirit (after we are saved) and should be kept in subjection to ghod and free of unclean things. As we have already mentioned, *"..... your body is the temple of the Holy Ghost..."* (I Cor. 6:19) Keep it clean!

* **The Tongue** can get you in a lot of trouble! Be careful how you use it! David said: *"..I will take heed to my ways, that I sin not with my tongue: I will keep my mouth with a bridle, ..."* (Ps. 39:1) Understand that every idle word that you speak will be revealed at the Judgment Seat of Christ.

* **People and places** can be your best friend or your worst enemy. The **people** with whom a Christian associates with and the **places** they go will determine their spiritual

> *"But I say unto you, That every idle word that men shall speak, they shall give account thereof in the day of judgment."* Matt. 12:36

condition. If you associate with people who are not living a Godly life, their bad habits will rub off on you! You cannot expect to quit some of your own bad habits if you hang around with those who still engage in them after you are saved. There is just not enough will power! The same goes for the places you go. It is simple! <u>Stay away from people and places of temptation or (bad influence) so that you may stay out of trouble that your spiritual growth not be hindered</u>.

This means to not have fellowship with lost people. *"Be ye not unequally yoked together with unbelievers: for what fellowship hath righteousness with unrighteousness? and what communion hath light with darkness? [15] And what concord hath Christ with Belial? or what part hath he that believeth with an infidel?"* (II Cor. 6:14-15)

And also, do not even fellowship with <u>Christians</u> who are not living right! *"Now we command you, brethren, in the name of our Lord Jesus Christ, that ye withdraw yourselves from every brother that walketh disorderly, and not after the tradition which he received of us. [7] For yourselves know how ye ought to follow us: for we behaved not ourselves disorderly among you;"* (II Thess. 3:6-7)

You can, however, deal with the lost to get them saved, or help the backslidden Christians to get them to repent and come back to Christ. You just can't <u>fellowship</u> with either. If they reject this attempt for help, you need to stay away from them; but continue to pray for them!

Since there is no way to be in fellowship with God while you frequent the wrong people and places, the key is to <u>replace</u> these bad elements from your past life with <u>Christian people and places</u>. Search until you find a good Bible believing church and involve yourself and your family in that work and with those Godly people.

A good rule for determining what you do, or the people and places you frequent, would be to ask yourself the question: "<u>would I do this if Jesus were here with me</u> in the flesh?"

Believe this: God will give you something better to replace what you give up for Him!

Well, you need to remember that you are indwelt with the Holy Spirit if you are saved, so He <u>is</u> with you! In fact, it is good to take this view about everything. Remember, *"The eyes of the Lord are in every place, beholding the evil and the good."* (Prov. 15:3)

Understandably, these are some of the hardest things the Christian must do, especially when first saved. Americans are used to being entertained, and it's hard to limit what you watch and read. Then, harder yet to change your lifestyle and the people and places you spend time with. **However, these are extremely important disciplines in the Christian life** and you will never grow enough spiritually to "walk in the Light" until you have control of these things.

In closing, here are some final thoughts on this subject. Jesus warned that the world would hate us (the born again child of God) just as it did Him! *"If the world hate you, ye know that it hated me before it hated you. [19] If ye were of the world, the world would love his own: but because ye are not of the world, but I have chosen you out of the world, therefore the world hateth you."* (John 15:18-19)

Notice in the scripture that Jesus said He had *"chosen us out of the world."* A good application of that verse is simply that He has called us out to be different. You became a new creature in Christ when you were saved (II Cor. 5:17). He wants us to be separate and set apart (sanctified) from the sins of this present world. **We are not to be partakers of the things others say is "alright" when God says they are wrong and sinful!**

We all know the world is full of temptation and has many things to covet and to occupy our minds if we are not careful. However, it is inexcusable for a "blood bought" Christian to allow the things of the world to come between them and the Lord Jesus Christ.

The scripture is very plain on this subject: *"Love not the world, neither the things that are in the world. If any man love the world, the love of the Father is not in him."* (I John 2:15) Where is your heart today? Is your time, your money and your mind consumed with your desire for the things, lusts, and pleasures of this world? Are you more concerned with the creation than the Creator? Whom do you love the most? Jesus, or the things of the world?

Is there any evidence in your life to prove you love Jesus above all else? **Or better put, is there even enough evidence in your life to convict you of being a "born again" Christian if you were on trial?**

Heed His instructions: *"Lay not up for yourselves treasures upon earth, where moth and rust doth corrupt, and where thieves break through and steal: [20] But lay up for yourselves treasures in heaven, where neither moth nor rust doth corrupt, and where thieves do not break through nor steal: [21] For where your treasure is, there will your heart be also."*(Matt. 6)

Chapter 6

Beware The Fellowship Killer #3

*Watch and pray, that ye enter not into temptation: the spirit indeed
is willing, but the flesh is weak.* Matt. 26:41

The Flesh

The "flesh" is another major enemy of the Christian. All
Christians will have trouble with the flesh sooner or later. With
most, it will be "sooner" rather than later! One key to your
fellowship with God is <u>how you handle the problems and
temptations of the flesh</u>. God understands the trials and
temptations of the flesh since He was here on earth and
experienced the same temptations we do, yet He remained sinless.
(Heb. 4:15)

Even the Apostle Paul, who was the greatest Christian to ever
live, had trouble with the flesh. *"For I know that in me (that is,
in my flesh,) dwelleth no good thing: for to will is present with
me; but how to perform that which is good I find not."* (Rom.
7:18) In other words, the spirit is willing but the flesh is weak!
Just like Paul, we are all rotten to begin with and must "crucify
the flesh daily" to overcome that "old nature" that still lives in us
and struggles for control. Although all who are saved are indwelt

with the Holy Spirit, the "old man" is still there just waiting to assert the old desires of the flesh. **If you are not filled with the Spirit there is room for something else to move in!** So, which ever one of these two natures you feed will be the strongest! Feed the godly nature that lives within you!

Although we can all expect some sort of trouble in the flesh because there is a constant war between the flesh and the Spirit, we need to be vigilant and stand ready to fight that which is contrary to God. *"For the flesh lusteth against the Spirit, and the Spirit against the flesh: and these are contrary the one to the other: so that ye cannot do the things that ye would."* (Gal. 5:17)

> *"So then they that are in the flesh cannot please God."* Rom. 8:8

First of all, let's define the word **"flesh."** This word has several meanings and different applications in which it is used. But, for the purpose of this lesson we are talking about the "flesh" as it applies to our physical desires, cravings, wants, lusts, coveting thoughts, and temptations. Meaning, the "things of the flesh" as opposed to "spiritual things." Some of these are specifically listed in the Bible. *"Now the works of the flesh are manifest, which are these; Adultery, fornication, uncleanness, lasciviousness, [20] Idolatry, witchcraft, hatred, variance, emulations, wrath, strife, seditions, heresies, [21] Envyings, murders, drunkenness, revellings, and such like: ....."* (Gal. 5:19-21)

These are sins of which the Christian should beware. God's Word says that we cannot please Him if we walk in the flesh. *"So*

then they that are in the flesh cannot please God." (Rom. 8:8)
Let's study these works of the flesh in more detail.

* **Desire and Lust (lasciviousness):** The desire for sexual
pleasure often grows to lust and then on to some sort of sexual
sin. Possibly, **the sin of adultery** (which is a married person
having sex with another), or **fornication** (which is any sex act
outside of marriage, including any homosexual act or unlawful
sexual intercourse).

If you put yourself in a position to be tempted in these types of
situations, you will probably end up doing something you would
not normally do. In the ungodly society wherein we now live,
these are things people engage in daily for pleasure with no
thought of God's commandments, nor the price they must pay for
these sins.

Once you are saved you are a new creature in Christ (II Cor. 5:17)
and are expected to live by His standards. It's tough, but you can
do it (with His help) and be happier in the process (Phil 4:13)! If
not, you will pay the price of God's chastisement! So, count the
cost before you knowingly sin. What do you stand to lose?

How do I avoid temptation? First, don't put yourself in the
position of being subjected to temptation, and you will avoid the
sin. Remember the chapter on the "World" about avoiding the
people (those unsaved or not living right), **places** (like bars,
worldly parties, etc.) and **things** (alcohol, drugs, etc.) that will
tempt you? Naturally, there are situations where single, godly
Christians are dating and are tempted, especially with respect to
fornication.

Obviously, you can never get to know each other well enough to be married if you don't spend some time together. But know this. If you honor your Savior's wishes and wait to have sexual relations, not only will the blessings be many, but also the bond between to two of you will be more solid. Plus, you miss the chastisement of the Lord for that sin, and avoid the damage to your fellowship with Him.

This is not as hard as it sounds if you saturate yourself with Jesus Christ, with the written word, and surround yourself with clean living people. You will be surprised how soon you will develop a new inner joy and peace that will replace those desires that were so important to the "old man" and the flesh. **When you reach the point that His desires for you are greater than your own desires, you are beginning to "walk in the Spirit" with the living God rather than the flesh.** You have arrived! At that juncture you will be amazed at how easy it is to reject the "old man" and his sinful ways. Try it!

* **Rebellion**: Idolatry, heresies, witchcraft and sedition are all some form of   rebellion against God and His written word. Idolatry, of course, is the worshipping of idols rather than worshipping God. An **idol** is generally envisioned as some man made statue,

> *For rebellion is as the sin of witchcraft, and stubbornness is as iniquity and idolatry.* I Sam. 15:23

figure, beads, picture or objects people use for worship. You can't worship God through these things! God is a spirit and must be worshipped as such! *"God is a Spirit: and they that worship him must worship him in spirit and in truth."* (John 4:24)

Understand that an idol is anything you put before God in your life. You need to stop here and think about this one! Your idol could be your work, hobbies, possessions, money or even your family. If it consumes more of your time, thoughts and energy, and if it is more important in your heart than your relationship with the Lord Jesus Christ, then it is an idol! Jesus demands to be number one in your life and if not: *"..be sure your sin will find you out."* (Num. 32:23) He just may take away the things you love more than you love Him! Think about that!

* **Heresies** are false teachings that are contrary to the Christian teachings of our Bible. The fundamental doctrines of the Christian faith are given by the Apostle Paul primarily in the New Testament books from Romans to Philemon. Paul, the Apostle to the Gentiles (anyone not a Jew) had some strong words for anyone teaching a false Gospel. *"But though we, or an angel from heaven, preach any other gospel unto you than that which we have preached unto you, let him be accursed."* (Galatians 1:8) **So this tells us that anyone teaching anything other than the shed blood and the finished work** (the Gospel, I Cor. 15:1-4) **of Jesus Christ for salvation is teaching heresy and is cursed!**

Study to shew thyself approved unto God, a workman that needeth not to be ashamed, rightly dividing the word of truth. II Tim. 2:15

The reason there are so many different denominations today is because of different doctrinal teachings regarding salvation. Salvation is obtained by

faith in His dying for you and then **receiving** (asking for) that **free gift** that gets you "born again." (Eph 2:8)

It is not any church, sacraments, water, nor anything you have to "do." **No one else has paid for your sins except for Jesus. Mohammed, Buddha, Confucius, and all the rest of the worlds' idols never paid for anyone's sin and can never get you to Heaven! If you have to pay for your own sin, you pay for it in the Lake of Fire! So, if you want to stay out of Hell, trust Jesus Christ and His shed blood plus nothing!** If, for some strange reason you want to go to Hell, then trust something or someone else! If you're not sure of your salvation, turn to the last page of this book before you continue and make sure!

That is the simplicity of salvation! (II Cor. 11:3) This may sound harsh, but this is something you better get straight (hopefully you already have) because there won't be a second chance. *"Jesus saith unto him, I am the way, the truth, and the life: no man cometh unto the Father, but by me."* (John 14:6) Also, you should never trust any book other than the Bible as your guide to salvation. No other book in the world has proven to be God's word by the fulfillment of hundreds of prophecies as has our Bible.

* **Sedition** is the act of stirring up rebellion against the government, civil authority, the law, or the administration of justice. In America, we have the freedom to speak out and to protest the things opon which we disagree. However, there are limits as to how far our actions can go before we are involved in an illegal act of civil disobedience.

God has commanded us to be in subjection to the powers that He has ordained. *"Let every soul be subject unto the higher powers. For there is no power but of God: the powers that be are ordained of God. [2] Whosoever therefore resisteth the power, resisteth the ordinance of God: and they that resist shall receive to themselves damnation."* (Rom. 13:1-2) Of course, when man's laws are contrary to God's Laws, it is time to pray about the matter. Also, you can exercise the freedom we have in this country to legally speak out and to petition the appropriate government bodies to bring about the necessary changes.

For example, Since abortion is against God's Law, Christians should peacefully demonstrate and canvas our government until laws are passed to make abortion illegal! It is not alright to blow up the abortion clinics or assassinate the doctors and those performing this act! Although we may sometimes have such feelings, that is the flesh and **not** the Spirit coming out in us.

This is, however, the unsaved liberals approach to things they don't like! *"Anything is alright if the end justifies the means!"* That action would put you in violation of God's Law and man's law. Another good verse on this subject is in I Peter. *"Submit yourselves to every ordinance of man for the Lord's sake: whether it be to the king, as supreme; [14] Or unto governors, as unto them*

And be not drunk with wine, wherein is excess; but be filled with the Spirit; Eph 5:18

that are sent by him for the punishment of evildoers, and for the praise of them that do well." (I Pet. 2:13-14)

* **Drunkenness and revellings** go hand in hand. Everyone knows what a drunk is. There are many people in our society who consume alcohol to the extent they are in a state of drunkenness on a regular basis. Some actually never completely sober- up, or rid the alcohol from their system before drinking more. It is a sad thing that some of these are actually professing Christians who, by doing this, are destroying their testimony, their health and are sinning against their own body. *"What? know ye not that your body is the temple of the Holy Ghost which is in you, which ye have of God, and ye are not your own? [20] For ye are bought with a price: therefore glorify God in your body, and in your spirit, which are God's."* (I Cor. 6:19-20)

Revellings means being wild, noisy, unruly, and disruptive. This description fits a lot of people, including most drunks who generally become worse the more drunk they become. Although drinking and drugs are not the only things that make people act this way, they are surely the most common. Unfortunately, there are some people who are this way by nature without the help of substances. Whatever the cause, the Lord does not like loud, boastful and unruly people.

Drunkenness and revellings will wreck your fellowship with the Lord and destroy your testimony to the extent that people may even go to hell because of your worldliness and sinfulness. It is just not worth it when you can be happier living clean and serving the Lord. The reason God uses so many people for His work who had a "rough past" is so others will see how being "born again" can truly change a person's heart, and make them much happier than they were in their sinful, godless life.

* Uncleanness, Envyings, and Murder. Being **unclean** can apply to being physically dirty, foul and filthy. Or, it can mean being morally impure, obscene or spiritually unclean according to religious laws. **Envy** is a feeling of discontent and desiring or coveting another's possessions, qualities, or advantages. (To envy another for what they are or for what they have.)

The Christian should learn to be content and thankful for what God has given him and not be concerned with that of another.

Murder, of course, is taking the life of another human being without justification. War is not murder. Taking the life of another in self defense is not murder. Capital punishment is not murder regardless of what the ungodly liberals say. In fact, the Bible teaches capital punishment in both the Old and the New Testament.

Now that we have briefly looked at some of the most obvious problems the flesh can present to the Christian, we need to sum it all up. The bottom line is that today's permissive society is a worldly society ruled by the flesh. Temptation is everywhere and is a dominant factor in almost every aspect of our daily lives.

It is almost impossible to avoid temptation as we go to work, shop, or attend public events. Moreover, sins of the flesh have become so common it almost seems :the norm" to do some of these things. Christians absolutely cannot allow themselves to be drawn into this trap of doing what "everyone else is doing."

Man has changed and become more tolerant of sin, but remember, God has not changed. **The rules are the same, and the price for**

disobedience and separating oneself from God are the same.
Hell is for the lost. Chastisement, loss of rewards and fruits of the
Spirit are reserved for the rebellious, backsliden Christian!

If you are to be in fellowship with God, you must apply His
commandments to your life and separate yourself from the world
and the sins of the flesh. Remember that there are sins of
"word," (something you say), **"thought"** (something you think),
and **"deed,"** (something you do). For example: ***"But I say unto
you, That whosoever looketh on a woman to lust after her hath
committed adultery with her already in his heart."*** (Matt. 5:28)
Notice, "with her." Both have sinned! The one that looked on
the woman to lust and the woman who invited the lust by her
actions or dress. The flesh must be constantly monitored to keep
it under subjection.

The fleshy fads of today such as: body piercing, tattoos, lipo
suction, botox, plastic surgery (for vanity's sake), are, for the
most part body worship and are contrary to God. ***"For they that
are after the flesh do mind the things of the flesh; but they that
are after the Spirit the things of the Spirit."*** (Rom. 8:5) As we
mentioned earlier, everything today is about "self" to the extreme
and to the exclusion of others.

There was a time not too far removed from today that people
were less self centered and more concerned for others. If your
neighbor was sick, you prepared meals for them and took care of
any chores or any other needs. Today many people don't even
know who their neighbor is, much less being concerned about
their needs. No time for anyone else, just self!

If you walk in the Spirit and the light of His presence the Lord will bless and reward you. *"There is therefore now no condemnation to them which are in Christ Jesus, who walk not after the flesh, but after the Spirit."* (Rom. 8:1) And if on the other hand, you as a born again child of God, reject His laws, you will pay the price. *"So then they that are in the flesh cannot please God."* (Rom. 8:8)

"Therefore, brethren, we are debtors, not to the flesh, to live after the flesh. [13]For if ye live after the flesh, ye shall die: but if ye through the Spirit do mortify the deeds of the body, ye shall live." (Rom. 8:12-13) The flesh must be crucified daily.

Now, there is nothing hard to understand about these plain verses from the written word of God. He has it worked out so that if you are a born again child of God, you cannot possibly be happy living after the world and the flesh in sin. Moreover, along with being miserable in this life, you will feel the whip of the Lord's chastisement because of your out of fellowship, backsliden condition. *"For whom the Lord loveth he chasteneth, and scourgeth every son whom he receiveth. [7] If ye endure chastening, God dealeth with you as with sons; for what son is he whom the father chasteneth not? [8] But if ye be without chastisement, whereof all are partakers, then are ye bastards, and not sons."* (Heb. 12:6-8)

Chapter 7

Beware The Fellowship Killer #4

Submit yourselves therefore to God. Resist the devil, and he will flee from you. James 4:7

The Devil

The devil is not some "make believe" red character with horns and a forked tail! He is not one to joke about; and his existence and motive, with respect to man, is certainly not a laughing matter. He (Satan) is the most powerful being in the universe outside of the God Head. He is the personification of evil, wickedness and ungodliness. His desire regarding man is to see all of us in the Lake of Fire! If you take him too lightly, he will lead you to hell and then laugh while you burn in that literal, physical, Lake of Fire forever! (Rev. 20:15)

He is the ultimate enemy! Regardless of what you have been told, you have little power over him other than to resist him with the armour of God (Eph. 6). Don't be foolish enough to believe that you can handle him alone! *"Submit yourselves therefore to God. Resist the devil, and he will flee from you."* (James 4:7) Study this short lesson and learn about this arch enemy of God Almighty. This is the one called the man of sin, the roaring lion, the beast and the son of perdition to name a few titles the Bible gives him.

The Devil (Satan, or Lucifer as he was originally called) is a created being. The same God that created man also created all of the heavenly creatures including Lucifer. The Bible speaks of Angels, Cherubims, and Seraphims. Although some preachers call all heavenly creatures angels, this is not Scriptural. The Bible plainly indicates a difference in these Heavenly creatures and to place them in one group is to show an unbelievable ignorance of the word of God.

Lucifer was a Cherub and not an angel as some would have you believe. He was not created as an angel, was never referred to as an angel in the Bible, and

> *Be sober, be vigilant; because your adversary the devil, as a roaring lion, walketh about, seeking whom he may devour:* I Pet. 5:8

never will be an angel! The Bible says he appears as an Angel of Light. It doesn't say he is an angel. We will deal with this issue later on in more detail.

"Thou art the anointed cherub that covereth; and I have set thee so: thou wast upon the holy mountain of God; thou hast walked up and down in the midst of the stones of fire. [15] Thou wast perfect in thy ways from the day that thou wast created, till iniquity was found in thee. [16] By the multitude of thy merchandise they have filled the midst of thee with violence, and thou hast sinned: therefore I will cast thee as profane out of the mountain of God: and I will destroy thee, O covering

cherub, from the midst of the stones of fire. [17] Thine heart was lifted up because of thy beauty, thou hast corrupted thy wisdom by reason of thy brightness: I will cast thee to the ground, I will lay thee before kings, that they may behold thee. [18] Thou hast defiled thy sanctuaries by the multitude of thine iniquities, by the iniquity of thy traffick; therefore will I bring forth a fire from the midst of thee, it shall devour thee, and I will bring thee to ashes upon the earth in the sight of all them that behold thee. [19] All they that know thee among the people shall be astonished at thee: thou shalt be a terror, and never shalt thou be any more." (Ezek. 28:14-19)

There, in just a few verses, you have a picture of the anointed cherub (Lucifer), his position, his fall from Heaven and his ultimate end. He will be joined in his final home (Rev.20:10) by all the false religions of the world, all the cults, all professing Christians teaching a false gospel (Gal. 1:8-9), all the Christ rejecting atheists, liberals and secular humanists. These, along with all those that put off being saved and die in their sin! Like most unsaved people today, his problem is his pride.

If you are unsaved, it is largely because of your pride, and the fact that you refuse to give up your sin and trust Jesus Christ as your Lord and Savior. You say, "No, that's not it, I just don't believe!" That's not right. The truth is you have not studied the book He left as a guide showing you how to get rid of your sin and to obtain eternal life! If you had, the Bible would have convicted you of sin and judgment to come. Or, maybe you are under conviction already and are just afraid you will have to give up something if you get saved.

Either way, you have rejected the One who died for your sins. Jesus said: *" Come unto me, all ye that labour and are heavy laden, and I will give you rest. [29] Take my yoke upon you, and learn of me; for I am meek and lowly in heart: and ye shall find rest unto your souls. [30] For my yoke is easy, and my burden is light."* (Matt. 11:28-30) And *"I am the way, the truth, and the life: no man cometh unto the Father, but by me."* (John 14:6) So get it right before it's too late! See the last page to learn how.

Lucifer was created as a beautiful and powerful creature. As the fifth cherub he covered the top of God's throne until he was cast down from that position because of his pride. *"How art thou fallen from heaven, O Lucifer, son of the morning! how art thou cut down to the ground, which didst weaken the nations! [13] For thou hast said in thine heart, I will ascend into heaven, I will exalt my throne above the stars of God: I will sit also upon the mount of the congregation, in the sides of the north: [14] I will ascend above the heights of the clouds; I will be like the most High. [15] Yet thou shalt be brought down to hell, to the sides of the pit."* (Isa. 14:12-15) The sad part here is that the Devil will take all unbelievers with him to that eternal Lake of Fire.

As we mentioned earlier, Lucifer was created as a cherub and not as an angel. So, what is the difference? A cherub has <u>four (4)</u> <u>faces</u> and <u>wings</u> while angels are <u>wingless</u> and always appear as <u>men</u> in the Bible. Although, angels are usually portrayed as having wings and being (sexless or sometimes female) by those ignorant of the Bible, this is not true. First we will look at some scripture about the cherubims. *[20] "This is the living creature that I saw under the God of Israel by the river of Chebar; and*

I knew that they were the cherubims. [21] Every one had four faces apiece, and every one four wings; and the likeness of the hands of a man was under their wings." (Ezek. 10:20-21)

As for the angels, they always show up as men in the Bible. Two angels appeared as men to Lot and warned him of the coming destruction of Sodom and Gomorrah in Genesis 19. Two more Angels appeared as men at the tomb of Jesus in Luke 24 and yet another two as men in Acts 1 as the Lord ascended up into Heaven. You will find more men as angels in Judges 13-15 and Revelation 21-22. They are always referred to as "men" or "he." So we see from Scripture that there is a big difference between angels and cherubims. Angels are not females, do not have wings, and are not sexless! Genesis chapter six is further evidence of that.

Seraphims are a little different than cherubims. *"Above it stood the seraphims: each one had six wings; with twain he covered his face, and with twain he covered his feet, and with twain he did fly. [3] And one cried unto another, and said, Holy, holy, holy, is the Lord of hosts: the whole earth is full of his glory. [4] And the posts of the door moved at the voice of him that cried, and the house was filled with smoke."* (Isa. 6:2-4)

Once again, these creatures are nothing like the men who appeared as angels. It is amazing that people accept as fact so many things they have heard about the Bible that just do not line up with Scripture. People simply believe things that they hear and pass them on without checking them out. That is why we are commanded to study the Scripture! (II Tim 2:15)

By nature, Satan is a deceiver. *"And the great dragon was cast out, that old serpent, called the Devil, and Satan, which deceiveth the whole world: he was cast out into the earth, and his angels were cast out with him."* (Rev. 12:9) He is a counterfeit. The one he envies and tries to counterfeit the most is the Lord Jesus Christ. *"Who opposeth and exalteth himself above all that is called God, or that is worshipped; so that he as God sitteth in the temple of God, shewing himself that he is God."* (II Thess. 2:4)

Satan desires worship! He was not satisfied with the great attributes and the position God gave him. He wanted to be equal with God and thought himself worthy of worship! Satan is king over all the children of pride. (Job 41:34) Satan is a false god. Because he is temporarily in control of this earth, he is called the "god of this world." *"But if our gospel be hid, it is hid to them that are lost: [4] In whom the god of this world hath blinded the minds of them which believe not, lest the light of the glorious gospel of Christ, who is the image of God, should shine unto them."* (II Cor. 4:3-4)

The Devil is in the business to deceive and to blind all that are lost so they will never come to a saving knowledge of Jesus Christ. He has many tricks and devices that he uses (along with the world

> *But if our gospel be hid, it is hid to them that are lost: 4 In whom the god of this world hath blinded the minds of them which believe not, lest the light of the glorious gospel of Christ, who is the image of God, should shine unto them.* II Cor. 4:2-4

and the flesh) to confuse, blind and damn the unsaved.

Satan is a thief! He will steal the word of God right out of your heart to keep you from being saved. ***"When any one heareth the word of the kingdom, and understandeth it not, then cometh the wicked one, and catcheth away that which was sown in his heart. This is he which received seed by the way side."*** (Matt. 13:19)

Satan also is a roaring lion! If you are already saved he will do his best to destroy your Christian life. His goal is to ruin your fellowship with the Lord and to destroy your personal testimony to the world. The last thing the Devil wants is for you to enjoy the fruits of the Spirit and to be a happy, soul winning Christian. He will stop at nothing to discourage you and make you a miserable backsliden Child of God. ***"Be sober, be vigilant; because your adversary the devil, as a roaring lion, walketh about, seeking whom he may devour:"*** (I Pet. 5:8)

His Devices: The devil has many tricks and devices, some of which have already been covered in chapters on the "World" and the "Flesh." But, other than his personal power, his greatest weapon is that he is not working alone. The Devil has plenty of help. He is the "prince of the air." He is the king over a multitude of other devils, unclean spirits, rulers of darkness and the spiritual wickedness in high places. ***"For we wrestle not against flesh and blood, but against principalities, against powers, against the rulers of the darkness of this world, against spiritual wickedness in high places."*** (Eph. 6:12) Your protection against the Devil and his workers of iniquity is the "armour of God." (See Ephesians chapter 6)

Where do all these demons and unclean spirits come from? The Bible is not clear on their origin, but most scholars agree that they are disembodied spirits. (In Mark 1:23, a devil is called an unclean spirit.) There is speculation they could have originated from the pre-Adamic race that perished between Genesis 1:1 and Genesis 1:2, or from the angels in Genesis six (6) mating with women and animals on earth. Some believe they are the fallen angels who rebelled against God with Lucifer, but this is unlikely because of the different way they are described in the Bible.

The fact is, it doesn't really matter from where they came, we know they are real! Jesus recognized them on several occasions in the Gospels and even spoke to them and cast them out. Another interesting thing was that when demons (devils) were confronted by Jesus, they knew who He was! *"And cried with a loud voice, and said, What have I to do with thee, Jesus, thou Son of the most high God? I adjure thee by God, that thou torment me not."* (Mark 5:7)

We know from Scripture these unclean spirits are intelligent beings with supernatural strength and knowledge. They can often accurately predict the future and can cause blindness, dumbness, insanity and suicidal tendencies. A person can be possessed by thousands (Mark 5:9) at a time, and animals can be possessed (Matt. 8:32). Demons are described as winged creatures and likened to fowls of the air. (Matt. 13, Mark 4, Rev. 18) There are also supernatural demoniac creatures in physical form coming up out of the bottomless pit in Revelation chapter 9. It is not known if these can travel around in spirit form or not, but it is a possibility.

Many people are hindered, and even possessed, by these unclean spirits and don't even realize it. They can affect the body as well as the mind. Contrary to popular belief, they can rule a Christian as well as a lost person! If you are not <u>filled</u> with the Spirit of God, there is room for something else! Besides, you don't have to be demon <u>possessed</u>, if one is siting on your shoulder and leading you by suggestion!

Unclean spirits are associated with excessive and compulsive behaviors such as: crying, nudity, suicidal tendencies, opposition to God and godly people, depression, drugs, alcohol, unspiritual music, pornography, insanity, lying, hatred, witchcraft, divination, sorcery, necromancy, (pretended communication with the dead) prognostication, magic and false doctrines, to name a few.

We are in a critical time in history from a spiritual standpoint. In these last days, demonic activity is at an all-time high. These devils and unclean spirits are even in many churches. *"Now the Spirit speaketh expressly, that in the latter times some shall depart from the faith, giving heed to seducing spirits, and doctrines of devils; [2] Speaking lies in hypocrisy; having their conscience seared with a hot iron; [3] Forbidding to marry, and commanding to abstain from meats, which God hath created to be received with thanksgiving of them which believe and know the truth."* (I Tim. 4:1-3)

They also control any and all religious groups that are not preaching and teaching the Gospel of Jesus Christ. (I Cor. 15:1-4) *"But though we, or an angel from heaven, preach any other gospel unto you than that which we have preached unto you, let*

91

him be accursed. " (Gal. 1:8)

Satan is also called the "dragon," the "beast," and the "son of perdition." He will rule the nations of this world for a short time in the not too distant future. Your only protection from him is to receive the Lord Jesus Christ as your Savior, walk in the Spirit of the living God with Him and put on the whole armor of God. (Eph.

Finally, my brethren, be strong in the Lord, and in the power of his might. 11 Put on the whole armour of God, that ye may be able to stand against the wiles of the devil. 12 For we wrestle not against flesh and blood, but against principalities, against powers, against the rulers of the darkness of this world, against spiritual wickedness in high places. Eph 6:10-12

6) Even if you are saved, you will be deceived and used of the devil without the armour.

Christians today are literally bombarded with the fiery darts of the Devil (Eph. 6) and the influences of demons (devils) and unclean spirits. They are often subtle, (as was the devil when he deceived Eve) and the Christian can be misled without realizing it. As we have mentioned in the lessons on the World and the Flesh, there are many things in and around us in our everyday lives that the powers of darkness use to weaken or destroy our Christian life. Satan was even able to reach the Apostles on occasion. (Luke 22:31-32) So don't be foolish enough to think he can't reach you!

His Last Hurrah: As we mentioned earlier, Satan wants worship and this desire (plus his pride) was the cause of his downfall. However, he will achieve his wish and will receive worship from some deceived nations of the earth for a short while during the Great Tribulation. In his physical form (a dragon at present) he is in the second heaven in that great body of water over our head (Ps. 148:4) called the great deep (Job 41). He will be cast down to earth and his angels with him in the near future. *"And the great dragon was cast out, that old serpent, called the Devil, and Satan, which deceiveth the whole world: he was cast out into the earth, and his angels were cast out with him."* (Rev. 12:9)

In Revelation 13:1, the second part of the unholy trinity shows up and the spirit of the devil enters the "beast." This is the anti-Christ (the son of perdition) who will take over a one world government and rule during the Tribulation. Satan will receive worship from the unsaved world (Rev. 13:4, 8) and cause everyone to receive a mark in their hand or forehead to be able to buy or sell. *"And he causeth all, both small and great, rich and poor, free and bond, to receive a mark in their right hand, or in their foreheads: [17] And that no man might buy or sell, save he that had the mark, or the name of the beast, or the number of his name."* (Rev. 13:16-17)

Those refusing to take the mark will be beheaded. *"[4]... and I saw the souls of them that were beheaded for the witness of Jesus, and for the word of God, and which had not worshipped the beast, neither his image, neither had received his mark upon their foreheads, ..."* (Rev 20:4)

And those who did take the mark were cast into hell! *"And the smoke of their torment ascendeth up for ever and ever: and they have no rest day nor night, who worship the beast and his image, and whosoever receiveth the mark of his name."* (Rev. 14:11)

After his reign, and at the end of the Tribulation, Satan will be chained for the one thousand year millennial reign of the Lord Jesus Christ. After this one thousand years of peace with Jesus on the throne in Jerusalem Jesus and the Christian saints will return to heaven and the Devil will be released for a little season, and then later cast into the Lake of Fire! *" And the devil that deceived them was cast into the lake of fire and brimstone, where the beast and the false prophet are, and shall be tormented day and night for ever and ever."* (Rev. 20:10)

This is the destiny of the one so many people are following in these last days. The unsaved will have the same end as their father the Devil! It seems almost unreal that so many will burn in Hell simply because they rejected the One (Jesus) who loved them the most and who suffered untold agony so they may live eternally with Him! This is the end result of pride! Will it be your end, or have you been saved?

It is doubtful you would have read this far in a book designed for Christians and not be saved. However, if that be the case, or if you are just not absolutely sure, now is the time to take care of it once and for all. In just a few seconds you can join the family of God and miss the eternal Lake of Fire with the Devil. If you want to be saved, stop here and turn to the last page in this book and we will show you God's simple plan of salvation!

Chapter 8

Beware The Fellowship Killer #5

What? know ye not that your body is the temple of the Holy Ghost which is in you, which ye have of God, and ye are not your own? I Cor. 6:19

Addictions

The word "addiction" automatically brings to mind "alcohol" or "drugs" to most of us. Although those are certainly the two most common and most devastating addictions in our society, there are many, many more addictions that hold people in bondage. What is an addiction? An addiction is when someone gives in to a strong desire or habit on a regular basis until they lose control. Addictions can become so strong and compelling that a person actually becomes a slave in bondage to their particular addiction.

Such bondage places the addiction in the forefront of the addict's life, and that becomes more important than anything else. They absolutely must satisfy that craving. The habit then consumes the person's time, thoughts, and energy to the extent that it becomes a god. Then eventually everything else in their life takes a back seat to the addiction.

Addictions come in various forms. It can be drugs, alcohol, sex, pornography, body image obsession, stealing, gambling, work or hobbies or almost anything that controls your life. Addiction controls the mind, will and emotions of a person. The person's very being (their soul) is in bondage.

The Cause: Some drugs and activities are so strong (with habit forming characteristics) that anyone who succumbs to them for any length of time becomes addicted. Naturally, there may be some difference in the time and quantity required for different individuals, but the end result is the same.

Then, there are the less addictive, but still dangerous drugs (along with alcohol) that seem to affect people differently. We know that some people have less resistance to certain things than others. For example, we have all known people who could use very little of a particular substance before showing signs of addiction. Others can use many times more of the same thing and simply quit when they are ready. Why is this?

There are many different opinions on why some people become addicted and are totally lose control, while others are less susceptible under the same conditions. There are speculations on genetic, psychological and even mental and emotional factors contributing to these differences.

A genetic tendency toward addictions (inherited from our ancesters) appears to be one of these causes. Similar body chemistry may well follow genetic lines making entire races or groups more susceptible to addiction with a particular substance than others. For example, we have always heard stories that the

American Indian cannot handle "firewater" (alcohol) and that it attacks the liver in this particular race of people more so than others. There is evidence that different races do have different traits and reactions to alcohol or drugs. Naturally, there are exceptions to every rule.

The body chemistry can also be different within the same groups or even families, at least in regards to their tolerance. For example even brothers and/or sisters may be different with respect to their

They call it dope because you are a dope if you take it! tolerance for a specific type of alcohol. It could be that each inherited traits from different parents. One may be able to drink beer in quantity, but have a low tolerance for whiskey, while the

other may have a high tolerance for whiskey. So, at least in some cases, even the different types of alcohol are a factor in the same genetic line. It stands to reason that the same could be true with respect to the different drugs.

Now, it comes down to this: whatever we put into our body must be dealt with by our own body chemistry whether it comes in through the mouth, lungs, blood, etc. If our particular body cannot properly deal with a substance, then the problem begins. Since the body chemistry affects the brain, this could also account for emotional and mental addictions. So, there are many possibilities and different aspects associated with the cause of addictions and many more variances among different people. But, it doesn't really matter becaues the cause is not the problem.

The bottom line is: don't participate and you cannot become

addicted, regardless of what your weakness may be! On the other hand, if you continue using drugs or alcohol you will eventually become addicted and/or destroy your health. People say, "I'll never go that far. It won't happen to me." But they do, and it does! It always starts with just a little. Many alcoholics started with beer and later graduated to the hard stuff.

Likewise, the drug addict often starts with smoking an occasional joint or two and then a little "recreational" cocaine, with a few pills here and there, and finally to "crack" cocaine and other hard core drugs. Bingo! You are addicted! So, what now??

You say, *"it's too late! I'm already addicted and I can't stop!"* Yes you can, but probably not by yourself! Regardless of the cause of your particular addiction you will need help! In many cases you will need more help than society and man can give you. You will need spiritual help to **permanently** solve your problem.

The Spiritual Element: There is more to the problem of addiction than meets the eye. Beyond the known factors we've mentioned, there is one more thing that is by far the most important. There is a spiritual element to addictions, and that element is what we are concerned with in this lesson. Why is the spiritual element so important? Because after twenty-five years of dealing with addicts of all kinds, the writer has seen a spiritual change work when the meetings, programs and all other methods have failed. Also, Jesus is proven to be the only permanent remedy.

Why is this? Because spirits are associated with drugs, alcohol, and other addictive elements. The powers of darkness use these weaknesses of the flesh. Most people don't know that the word "pharmacy," (where legal drugs come from) or "pharmaceutical" is from a Greek word linked to the practice of witchcraft. The Greek word for "sorcery" literally means "drugs."

Drug addiction is a common element in the practice of witchcraft and Devil worship, thus, the spiritual link. If you are fooling with drugs and alcohol, you are subjecting yourself to the spirit world and the powers of darkness. (Eph. 6) You can literally open the door for unclean spirits to come in and control you to some degree. For example almost everyone has done something under the influence of alcohol or drugs that they would not have normally done without the substance. This is not just impaired judgment. You are simply weak, and your judgment is easily altered by outside influences. To correct the spiritual part of the problem, you must make spiritual changes.

After twenty-five years of working with addicts, I can promise you that once addicted, it will take the work of the Holy Spirit to get you off of the "stuff" and keep you off. The "meetings" and "programs" may be of some help initially. However, you will never have closure, nor be able to put the addiction behind you until you cease to fellowship with addicts and stop frequenting the places they do! Otherwise, you are constantly reminded of your problem!

You can't put it behind you and move on with the plan God has for your life if you are talking and thinking about your addiction all the time and hanging around those with the same problem!! Granted, this is hard to do, but these changes are necessary to put it completely out of your life.

The Remedy: So, if you want to ever have victory over your addiction, the first step is to get saved! Then, you are a new creature in Christ (II Cor. 5:17) equiped with the indwelling Holy Spirit of God. You can now begin a new life without the substance to which you were addicted to and without the people and places that go with it! If you are already saved and in this condition, you need to repent (I John 1:9), recommit your life to Jesus Christ and surrender all to Him!

Will being saved guarantee your cure? Not necessarily. It will give you the power (through the Holy Spirit) and ability to achieve the victory over your addiction, but you must do your part. Many Christians never receive complete victory over their addiction because they have not totally surrendered the problem to Christ. You must completely turn away from the substance, the people and the places that tempt you because, by association they keep the substance in the forefront of your mind. Then, with the physical temptation removed, the Holy Spirit will begin to heal the mind and body so you will not need the substance.

> *This I say then, Walk in the Spirit, and ye shall not fulfil the lust of the flesh. 17 For the flesh lusteth against the Spirit, and the Spirit against the flesh: and these are contrary the one to the other: so that ye cannot do the things that ye would.* Gal 5:16-17

It will not be easy. You will have to saturate yourself with the word of God, establish a close relationship with Jesus Christ, and develop a good prayer life to succeed. You need to find a Bible believing, soul winning church and be involved in that work to keep you busy. You will find that serving the Lord and associating with godly people will help you get your mind off the emotional and physical cravings your body feels for the substance you abused.

This new life will make you feel so much better about yourself and will give you more confidence than you can imagine. But remember. Jesus can only help you solve your problem and give you the greatest joy you've ever had if you truly surrender it all to Him and seek His will in your life. I know it works because I have "been there and done that," and He has kept me for twenty-nine years because I gave it all to Him.

I said earlier that if you are an addict and you are already saved, you need to repent and recommit your life to Jesus Christ, and confess (I John 1:9) to get your sins under the blood and return to fellowship with God.

Chapter 9

Beware The Fellowship Killer #6

"Because that, when they knew God, they glorified him not as God, neither were thankful; but became vain in their imaginations, and their foolish heart was darkened." Rom. 1:21

Imaginations And Fantasies

It has been said many times that **"you are what you eat."** This, I believe, is not the case. Although, what you eat can surely affect your physical body, and even your health, it can never constitute the real you. This phrase was coined by a secular, humanistic world concerned with life in the flesh, while little thought is given by modern man to his spiritual condition. Modern man is consumed with his physical appearance, abilities, wealth and achievement, and therein lies the primary focus of the thoughts and intents of his heart.

A more accurate statement is that **"you are what you think."** The real you is your soul, your mind, will and emotions. Consequently, it is your imaginations, fantasies, thoughts and intents of the heart that determine who you are, what you are and who or what ultimately controls your life! What do you dwell on the most in your own thought process? Now, if you are honest you will admit that there are many corrupt fantasies and wicked imaginations that you entertain in thought from time to time.

After many years of counseling on these matters, I am convinced this subject is one of the biggest hindrances to spiritual growth among God's people today. **Some of you, although born again, are letting your imaginations and fantasies affect your spiritual condition and your relationship with the Lord Jesus Christ**. Hopefully, this lesson will be of some help in correcting that problem.

At this point in examining "fellowship killers" the reader should have digested ample material to understand the dangers of entertaining worldly thoughts and standards. Once saved, you became a new creature in Christ, but if you are not careful with what occupies your heart and mind, your spiritual condition will rocket right back into the worldly cesspool. There is no need for that to happen if you understand the many snares and pitfalls associated with this problem and how to deal with them.

In this chapter we will peruse some history of man's departure from God brought about by his sinful, self-serving imaginations. We will also attempt to make you more aware of how your own thoughts can affect your spiritual condition and how to avoid the problems that can result.

Now to begin with, not all imaginations are bad. In fact, imaginations can be good, healthy and fruitful to the individual and to mankind in general if channeled in the right direction. If not for imaginations there would be no preachers, evangelists or missionaries. Also, we would still be living in the "Dark Ages" with respect to all the modern inventions and conveniences we enjoy every day. And most important of all, we would not have a Bible in English if some had not heeded God's call and imagined in their hearts to complete the work.

So, if your imaginations are centered around loving and serving the Lord Jesus Christ and bringing others to a saving knowledge of Him, and good things in general, you are in good shape. However, from the beginning, the tendency of man has been to pursue the evil rather than the good, and that is the focus of this lesson.

What history reveals: From the beginning, man has been in trouble with God because of his imaginations and the intents of his heart. *".....for the imagination of man's heart is evil from his youth; ...."* (Gen. 8:21) Eve ignored what God said and

Your thoughts today can be the road map to your actions tomorrow, so be careful!

allowed Satan to corrupt her thought process and thereby making her think it would be okay, or even good, to eat the forbidden fruit. Cain was so jealous of Abel that he allowed his thoughts to lead him to murder his own brother.

Obviously, Satan has been at work from the beginning using our thoughts, imaginations and fantasies to derail our fellowship with God and ruin our lives! Welcome to the cesspool of earth after the fall of Adam and Eve!

Things got even worse as time went by .*"And God saw that the wickedness of man was great in the earth, and that every imagination of the thoughts of his heart was only evil continually. [6] And it repented the Lord that he had made man on the earth, and it grieved him at his heart. [7] And the Lord said, I will destroy man whom I have created from the face of the earth; both man, and beast, and the creeping thing, and the fowls of the air; for it repenteth me that I have made them.* (Gen.6:5-7)

Here we see the full ramification of evil imaginations and how the end result is death. It would be a terrible thing to know that your own thoughts and imaginations caused God to be sorry He even made you and wanted to destroy you! Man is forever making the mistake of depending on his own thoughts, intelligence and wisdom to guide him, and the result is always the same! Disaster! *"For the wisdom of this world is foolishness with God. ...."* (I Cor. 3:19) It always has been and always will be!! So if we are to learn anything from the history of man and his relationship with God, and how to avoid the pitfalls of our own thoughts, we will glean it from the Bible and through fervent prayer.

Modern Man

Some things never change! **Man's course was set against and away from God early on, and will remain that way until it all winds up at the Great White Throne Judgment!**

As we all know, the spirit is often willing, but the flesh is weak.

Meanwhile, sinful and wicked imaginations are more prevalent today than ever before. With all the focus on sex and violence in the media: movies, TV, books,

105

pornography, internet and body worship, it is increasingly hard for the child of God to avoid exposure. When subjected to so much of this on such a regular basis, it is hard for the Christian not to give in to temptation. Therefore, the ungodly things one sees and hears every day in the secular world can only signal trouble for the unprepared Christian.

On the list of seven things the Bible says God hates is **"wicked imaginations!"** *"These six things doth the Lord hate: yea, seven are an abomination unto him: [17] A proud look, a lying tongue, and hands that shed innocent blood, [18] An heart that deviseth wicked imaginations, feet that be swift in running to mischief, [19] A false witness that speaketh lies, and he that soweth discord among brethren."* (Prov. 6:16-19)

Are your own thoughts and imaginations a current or potential problem in your present spiritual life? If so, you need to gain control of your thinking process before it escalates to the point that you have serious problems. And it will! I've been told. *"I know my thoughts and imaginations are probably sinful, but I enjoy my fantasies and no one knows about them but me, so how can it hurt?"* It can and will! *"Be sure your sin will find you out!"* (Num. 32:23)

How You Get Hooked

Although somewhat redundant, we will reiterate what we have said in previous chapters because of it's extreme importance. The eyes and ears are the doorway to the soul. What we see, hear and imagine are seeds for thoughts easily planted in the mind! **So first of all, be very careful with your eyes!** Sometimes it is necessary to look away rather than record something with your eyes that will cause you to sin. **Ditto, what you hear!** Refuse to listen to any garbage that will get you thinking along lines you should avoid.

The Bible addresses the eye problem! *"Having eyes full of adultery, and that cannot cease from sin; beguiling unstable souls: ......"* (II Pet. 2:14) *For all that is in the world, the lust of the flesh, and the lust of the eyes, and the pride of life, is not of the Father, but is of the world.* (1 John 2:16)   Your own imaginations can also be part of the problem.

Granted, you can't always control what pops into your mind, given what we are all exposed to daily in this rotten world. But, we can control whether or not we allow our mind to <u>dwell</u> on a sinful thought. If you dwell on it, your imagination will build around that thought until you find yourself in a fantasy of sin.

Consider also, that along with the natural tendencies of the flesh and the "old man" to sin, there are spiritual powers at work twenty-four hours a day, seven days a week, trying to destroy your Christian life. If the powers of darkness and the ever present, unclean spirits can manipulate your thinking, your Christian life will soon be in shambles. You will not only lose the fruits of the Spirit (and be a miserable

You don't have to be actually possessed by the Devil to be under his control!

child of God) but also your usefulness for Him will also be neutralized.

Don't be deceived! Although some say that a Christian cannot be controlled by the Devil, that is a false teaching! You can be saved and indwelt by the Holy Spirit, but not be <u>filled</u> with the Spirit! If you are not <u>filled</u> with the Spirit there is room for something else! Whether or not you can actually be possessed by an unclean spirit is irrelevant!

If the Devil is active in your thought process or planting thoughts for you to entertain, and if you go along for the enjoyment, your spiritual downfall has already been set in motion. You may not realize it, but you are being led, and to some degree controlled. Although it may take several years to develop, it will eventually slip up on you and reach the point where you lose control along with the will to repent and return to fellowship with God.

Where It Can Lead

If sinful imaginations and fantasies go unchecked, they become addictions. You just had a whole chapter on this subject so I will not belabor it here. But remember, **addictions can become so strong and compelling that a person actually becomes a slave in bondage to their particular addiction, therefore beguiling the soul.** (II Pet. 2:14)

Naturally, the more advanced the sinful condition is, the harder it is to get rid of it and return to that sweet fellowship with God that we all need. So, the key for the Christian is to not let sinful thoughts, inmaginations and fantasies get that inital foothold. How can I do this?

Avoiding The Problem

As mentioned earlier, our thoughts are formed by things we see, hear and imagine. The mind deals with hundreds (if not thousands) of thoughts each day. Some are just a passing flash in the mind, while there are others on which we dwell. The unclean or sinful ones can come from any source. However, the ones that cause us the most trouble are often the same ones that gave us problems when we were lost.

> *Just about the time you think you have the victory over your old sins one or more will pop up again in your Christian life looking for furtile ground in which to take root.*

Be careful not to give any ground to the sinful thoughts that flash into your mind ocassionally. And they will! Although we cannot always control what does pop up in the mind, if we don't entertain the thought and dwell on it, then that thought cannot take root! **Every problem with imaginations that the Christian has began somewhere back down the line as a sinful thought that was dwelt opon and magnified by feeding it!**

So, when a bad thought pops up, **immediately** put it out of your mind. Isolate it, and starve it to death! If you catch yourself unwittingly entertaining and feeding the thought, stop immediately and ask the Lord for forgivness. Ask Him to take over your subconcious mind and help you to quickly recognize and to discard the sinful thought.

The Apostle Paul gave us some good advice along these lines. *"Casting down imaginations, and every high thing that exalteth itself against the knowledge of God, and bringing into captivity every thought to the obedience of Christ;"* (II Cor. 10:5) Cast the bad thoughts out and bring them all under control in obedience to the Lord Jesus Christ!

Feed the mind with spiritual thoughts and *"Submit yourselves therefore to God. Resist the devil, and he will flee from you. [8] Draw nigh to God, and he will draw nigh to you. Cleanse your hands, ye sinners; and purify your hearts, ye double minded."* (James 4:7-8)

Where do you personally stand on this subject? Remember: *"Therefore to him that knoweth to do good, and doeth it not, to him it is sin. "* (James 4:17)

Paul brings it all together in his letter to the Phillippians: *"Finally, brethren, whatsoever things are true, whatsoever things are honest, whatsoever things are just, whatsoever things are pure, whatsoever things are lovely, whatsoever things are of good report; if there be any virtue, and if there be any praise, think on these things."* (Phil.4:8) May all your thoughts and imaginations glorify God! Now we will look at another subject that can affect your spititual condition.

Be patient! We are getting there!

Chapter 10

Beware The Fellowship Killer #7

"Love not the world, neither the things that are in the world. If any man love the world, the love of the Father is not in him." I John 2:15

Separation

One of the greatest challenges for Christians (especially new Christians) is the Bible doctrine of separation. It is one of the most important doctrines of the New Testament. It is a characteristic of a holy and righteous God who is not tolerant of any degree of sin. Nor does He expect us to be! As His children, we are expected to stay away from sinful and ungodly people, places, and things. The Bible says in I Pet. 1:15-16, *"But as he which hath called you is holy, so be ye holy in all manner of conversation; Because it is written, Be ye holy; for I am holy."* That should be our goal.

Our spiritual condition, our fellowship with God and our usefulness to Him are contingent upon, and can be measured by, our degree of separation from the world. So, we are given clear instructions on where to place our love and affections: *"If ye then be risen with Christ, seek those things which are above, where Christ sitteth on the right hand of God. [2] Set your affection on things above, not on things on the earth. [3] For ye are dead, and your life is hid with Christ in God."* (Col. 3:1-3)

It seems that in today's times most Christians are unconcerned about separation and few really practice it. It must grieve God's heart to see this disobedience in His people and the damage it is doing to their spiritual condition. Every child of God should take time to examine each fellowship and association with others, in light of God's word on this subject. Then the necessary changes should be made to mend the broken fellowship with **Him**.

In this chapter we will show different aspects of separation in the Bible and point out the dangers of **not** being obedient to God in this doctrine. You will notice as we progress in the subject that God is firm in His instructions on separation from ungodliness. Ungodliness can be found almost anywhere. It can be found among unbelievers, believers and Christian organizations or ministries which are disobedient to the Word of God!

Separate from False Teachers

Our Lord has warned us about false teachers and those who would spread false doctrine in II Pet. 2:1-17. *"But there were false prophets also among the people, even as there shall be false teachers among you, who privily shall bring in damnable heresies, even denying the Lord that bought them, and bring upon themselves swift destruction. [2] And many shall follow their pernicious ways: .... [17] These are wells without water, clouds that are carried with a tempest; to whom the mist of darkness is reserved for ever."*

A well without water is a worthless well!! Therefore, a false teacher or prophet is worthless to all, and a hindrance to the Christian's spiritual growth. Actually, false teachers are non-believers since they have ignored or perverted the true Gospel of Christ!

The Apostle Paul, the greatest Christian who ever lived, had some strong words to say to those who would pervert the Gospel of Christ. *"I marvel that ye are so soon removed from him that called you into the grace of Christ unto another gospel: [7] Which is not another; but there be some that trouble you, and would pervert the gospel of Christ. [8] But though we, or an angel from heaven, preach any other gospel unto you than that which we have preached unto you, let him be accursed. [9] As we said before, so say I now again, If any man preach any other gospel unto you than that ye have received, let him be accursed. [10] For do I now persuade men, or God? or do I seek to please men? for if I yet pleased men, I should not be the servant of Christ."* (Gal. 1:6-10)

> **My doctrine is not mine, but his that sent me. 17 If any man will do his will, he shall know of the doctrine, whether it be of God, or whether I speak of myself.** John 7:16-17

Notice that the Apostle Paul repeated the same statement twice so you would not miss it! It was a rather strong statement, too! Now you can see that God considers it an awful thing for anyone to reject Bible truth. The world today is full of those who change, pervert or twist the Scripture and take it out of context to try to make it say what they want it to say.

113

One way to spot false teaching is that it invariability makes the Bible contradict itself, whereas rightly dividing the word (II Tim. 2:15) never will. You must remember to always interpret unclear verses in light of the verses that are clear and plain; not the other way around!

For do I now persuade men, or God? or do I seek to please men? for if I yet pleased men, I should not be the servant of Christ." Gal. 1:10

What should you do if someone is teaching false doctrine? First, know that it is the Holy Spirits job to reveal it to him and not you. Therefore, if he is willing to sit down and search the scriptures in the proper context with you, he may see the light. If he is not willing to listen or see the truth, we are instructed to leave him alone.

Tit. 3:9 says: *"But avoid foolish questions, and genealogies, and contentions, and strivings about the law; for they are unprofitable and vain. [10] A man that is an heretick after the first and second admonition reject; [11] Knowing that he that is such is subverted, and sinneth, being condemned of himself."* (Tit. 3:9-11)

As a Christian, you should never join together with any man, group or organization that has rejected the plain Bible teachings on the Gospel of Jesus Christ under the New Testament Covenant.

In II Cor. 6:14-18 we are admonished: *"Be ye not unequally yoked together with unbelievers: for what fellowship hath*

114

righteousness with unrighteousness? and what communion hath light with darkness? [15] And what concord hath Christ with Belial? or what part hath he that believeth with an infidel? [16] And what agreement hath the temple of God with idols? for ye are the temple of the living God; as God hath said, I will dwell in them, and walk in them; and I will be their God, and they shall be my people. [17] Wherefore come out from among them, and be ye separate, saith the Lord, and touch not the unclean thing; and I will receive you, [18] And will be a Father unto you, and ye shall be my sons and daughters, saith the Lord Almighty."

Is that plain enough?? If you want fellowship with God, you simply cannot ignore the wickedness of unbelief and false teaching. If you are in any way connected with either, get away from it, confess your past association as sin and ask God's forgiveness. Don't let the peer pressure of man keep you unequally yoked together with someone or some thing that will separate you from fellowship with God.

Separating From Wayward Brethren

This is the tough one! Most Christians don't find it that hard to avoid fellowship with false teachers when they recognize them, and most also understand the necessity to avoid a worldly lifestyle. However, it is much more difficult sometimes to separate from disobedient brethren. The backslidden and disobedient one may, in fact, be a close friend or family member.

Nevertheless, we are told not to walk in fellowship with them. II Thessalonians chapter three speaks to this. *"Now we command you, brethren, in the name of our Lord Jesus Christ, that ye withdraw yourselves from every brother that walketh disorderly, and not after the tradition which he received of us. [7] For yourselves know how ye ought to follow us: for we behaved not ourselves disorderly among you;* (II Thess. 3:6-7) ....[11] *For we hear that there are some which walk among you disorderly, working not at all, but are busybodies. .... [14] And if any man obey not our word by this epistle, note that man, and <u>have no company with him</u>, that he may be ashamed. [15] Yet count him not as an enemy, but admonish him as a brother.*

Here we are told to separate from those who are disorderly and/or busybodies. You admonish him in love as a brother, but you must break any fellowship with him until he straightens up. If you don't spend time with him, then the bad habits and wrong-doings won't rub off on you! God is serious about separation. Read on.

"Your glorying is not good. Know ye not that a little leaven leaveneth the whole lump? [7] Purge out therefore the old leaven, that ye may be a new lump, as ye are unleavened. For even Christ our passover is sacrificed for us: ....[9] I wrote unto you in an epistle not to company with fornicators: [10] Yet not altogether with the fornicators of this world, or with the covetous, or extortioners, or with idolaters; for then must ye needs go out of the world. [11] But now I have written unto you not to keep company, if any man that is called a brother be a fornicator, or covetous, or an idolater, or a railer, or a drunkard, or an extortioner; with such an one no not to eat. .... 13] [But them that are without God judgeth. <u>Therefore put away from among yourselves that wicked person</u>." (I Cor. 5:6-13)

Like leaven, a "little" sin goes a long way. If you subject yourself
to any degree of it, even just being around a person or a place that
puts you in temptation's way, you too will fall!!! Then there is
your Christian testimony. *"You are known by the company you
keep." Do not be foolish enough to think you may be the
exception to the rule and you can handle the situation.* Many
have learned the hard way about the necessity of separation. *Just
avoid these people, places, and things that will tempt you and
God will bless your effort!* Remember, you are "blood bought"
and belong to HIM, if you are saved.

Although all the chapters are necessary to prepare the Christian
for that close fellowship of "walking in His light," the next one is,
without a doubt, one of the more valuable and necessary ones.
Spend some time there and determine what areas wherein you
need improvement.

Growing With Prayer

"And when he looked on him, he was afraid, and said, What is it, Lord? And he said unto him, Thy prayers and thine alms are come up for a memorial before God." Acts 10:4

Someone said God's telephone number is Jeremiah 33:3: *"Call unto me, and I will answer thee, and shew thee great and mighty things, which thou knowest not."*

Sadly, few of God's people call on Him as often as they should, and few have a prayer life that is pleasing to our Lord. Likely,this is because most don't understand the **need for** or the **power** and **reward** associated with a good prayer life. God is anxious to hear from you! Have you called on Him lately? The Bible says: *"I will therefore that men pray every where."* (I Tim. 2:8)

Hopefully, you have. However, many Christians today use prayer only for emergency. They seldom pray unless they want something or need God in times of trouble. It is amazing that folks expect God to give what they ask for under these conditions. It's also sad that these types of Christians spend their whole life without experiencing the awesome power of prayer.

Neither do they experience the nearness it brings one to God. If you are saved and your prayer life needs improvement, this chapter is for you. Hopefully, it will help you better understand the various aspects of prayer and what God expects of you. If you are unsaved, read on to find out how you can be saved.

What is Prayer?

Prayer is the medium through which we express our feelings, needs, desires and thanks to our God. It is also the way He has provided for us to make intercessions for others. Prayer and the word of God, are without question, the two most powerful tools in the universe. James 5:16 says; *"...The effectual fervent prayer of a righteous man availeth much."* So, obviously there is much power available to a Christian through prayer. However, we must understand that there is much more to it than simply asking for something we want. How we pray is important to our Lord, and the child of God should be anxious to learn what God expects and then strive to please Him.

Importance Of Prayer

Prayer is important for several reasons. First of all, it is God's will that we spiritually come into His presence and communicate with Him! It is the starting block of fellowship and walking in the light. *"I will therefore that men pray every where."* (I Tim. 2:8) *"Pray without ceasing."* (I Thess. 5:17) *".....Men ought always to pray and not faint."* (Luke 18:1) These verses make it plain that God desires and expects us to pray on a regular basis.

The Bible says David was a man after God's own heart! Would you like God to say that about you? Well, one of the reasons that

119

David found favor in the eyes of the Lord was because of his prayer life. Read through the Psalms which David wrote to get an idea how he communicated with the Lord. David thought prayer was important and prayed at least three times a day: *"Evening, and morning, and at noon, will I pray, and cry aloud: and he shall hear my voice."* (Ps. 55:17)

The Way To Pray

One of the disciples asked Jesus: *"Lord, teach us to pray...."* (Luke 11:1). That is how you too should begin. Ask for His help! Here are some things that can serve as a guide; however, the **Holy Spirit is the real teacher.**

1) Confession: Christians sin, and that sin separates you from fellowship with God! *"If we say that we have not sinned,we make him a liar, and his*

"Pray without ceasing." I Thess. 5:17

word is not in us." (I John 1:10) It is absolutely necessary that you repent and confess any sins of word, thought or deed that you have committed. **If you are saved, you belong to Him. Therefore, when you sin you lose fellowship (not salvation) with the Father. Then, sincere repentance and confession are necessary to restore that fellowship.**

The first chapter of I John is about fellowship with God. It says in verse 7: *"But if we walk in the light, as he is in the light, we have fellowship one with another, and the blood of Jesus Christ his Son cleanseth us from all sin."* Walking in the light means to not sin! But if we do sin, He gives us a promise of forgiveness in V9 if we confess that sin: *"If we confess our sins, he is faithful and just to forgive us our sins, and to cleanse us from all unrighteousness."* Notice that He said **ALL** unrighteousness.

2) Thankfulness: *"In everything give thanks: for this is the will of God in Christ Jesus concerning you."* (I The. 5:18) We should give thanks to God for the many blessings of this life. A few of those blessings that we often take for granted are: our health, our family, our job, our success in life, our home and our possessions (which God has so generously provided).

And don't forget the most important blessing of all...our salvation and our Saviour, the Lord Jesus Christ. Notice the word *"everything"* in the verse. That word covers all the good and all the bad. Give thanks for the bad, as the verse says, and even take it a step farther and praise Him for it. Sound strange? This is discussed more in the next section.

3) Praise: Always, always, remember to praise God. He loves to be worshipped and praised for who He is, and what He has done for us! David says in Psalms 34:1 *"I will bless the Lord at all times: his praise shall continually be in my mouth."* Praise Him not only for all the good things in your life and for our Saviour, but praise Him for the hard times, troubles and setbacks in life! Yes. That's right!

These are building blocks. Know that nothing happens in a Christian's life that God Himself doesn't orchestrate or a least allow it to happen for a reason. Although praising Him in these cases may be hard to do, it lets God know that <u>you are in submission to Him</u> and to His will in your life. In so doing, you have opened the door for spiritual growth and to be molded and shaped by God for His purpose and use. Remember, there is always a reason why Christians suffer. So praise Him for the bad and the good, knowing that your Lord is trying to prepare you for something He has in store for you in the future.

4) Supplication: *"....but in everything by prayer and supplication with thanksgiving let your request be made known unto God."* (Phil. 4:6) This is the "request" part of your prayer. It should include the **wants**, **needs** and the **desires** of your heart. Ask for what you want, but don't ask for something you know is wrong or that you know may be bad for you in the long run. Simply express your feelings (He knows them anyway) and leave it up to the Lord's will. It's also important you remember to put others on the top of your prayer list. In other words, don't just always be praying for yourself! Rather, be generous in your prayers for others.

We are to be intercessors for those in need, asking God to intervene and to help them. You should even pray for those who have wronged you, and be **quick to forgive** them. The Bible says: *"And when ye stand praying, forgive, if ye have ought against any..."* (Mk. 11:25)

Although it may be hard, learn to **pray for your enemies**. *".....Bless them that curse you..."* (Matt. 5:44) Also, we must **pray in faith**, believing God will deliver. *"But let him ask in faith, nothing wavering. For he that wavereth is like a wave of the sea driven with the wind and tossed. For let not that man think that he shall receive any thing of the Lord."* (James 1:6-7) See also Hebrews 11:6: *"...for he that cometh to God must* *believe that he is, and that he is a <u>rewarder of them</u> that diligently seek him."*

Next, your requests should always be concluded with the request that **God's will** (and not yours) be done in the matters which you have petitioned Him. Jesus prayed to the Father, *"Not my will, but thine be done."* If you need more grace to handle "no" for an answer, then ask for it. In addition, **pray out loud**. Not for others to hear, but a quiet communication between you and God. Remember, Jesus created the earth and universe with the spoken word. So, obviously, there is great power in the spoken word!

Finally, your prayers should always be **in the Spirit** (Eph. 6:18) **directed to the Father** (Acts 12: 5) **in the name of Jesus Christ.** (John 14:13)

5) Listen to God: When you are praying you are speaking to God. Be aware that He may be speaking back to you. So, listen with your heart as He impresses on you His desires. It is important at these times to be sure you are hearing the Holy Spirit and not an unclean counterfeit spirit. Be aware that Satan will try to interfere with your prayer life because he doesn't want you praying and receiving it's benefits. So, *"..try the spirits whether they be of God"* (I John 4:1)

Remember, the Holy Ghost will **never** contradict the word of God. Therefore, anything contrary to the word is the wrong spirit.

Secondly, prayer is **the way to unleash the power** we have in Christ through the Holy Ghost. Our God is a God of miracles and is eager to release that power within His will. However, be careful for what you ask. God may give it to you just about the time you realize that your request was the last thing in this world you really needed!

Why Prayers Are Not Answered

Actually, prayers are always answered, it's just that many times the answer is NO! We tend to think that if we don't get an affirmative answer, then we didn't get one at all. This, of course, is not the case. Here are some reasons we don't have our prayers answered our way.

> *"The eyes of the Lord are over the righteous, and his ears are open unto their cry."* (I Pet. 3:12)

Disobedience: If you do not obey God and try to live a life that is pleasing to Him, how can you expect Him to give you what you want? If you have children of your own, do you give them everything they want? Of course not! And when they are disobedient you are not likely to give them much of anything! Amen? Why should God treat you any differently? The Bible says: *"And whatsoever we ask, we receive of him, because we keep his commandments, and do those things that are pleasing in his sight."* (I John 3:22)

Are you keeping His commandments? Here is another one. *"But your iniquities have separated between you and your God, and your sins have hid his face from you, that he will not hear."* (Isa. 59:2) If you have any unconfessed sin, forget it! Don't waste your breath. That is, until you get rid of the sin! How do you get rid of the sin? The entire chapter of I John 1 is on fellowship with God. If you have unconfessed sins of word, thought or deed, then repent, confess and ask for His forgiveness to get it under the blood! Read "# **1)** about Confession" again.

Wrong reasons: Do not expect God to honor your requests if you are asking for self-serving reasons. Most of your prayers should be for others anyway. Some people seem to think that God is some great big "Santa Claus" just waiting to give you wealth and all the rich blessings of this life. The "name it and claim it" garbage being taught today by some people is unscriptural.

In fact, this false doctrine is totally opposite of what the word of God teaches. Jesus said not to lay up treasures on earth, but rather in Heaven. (Matt. 6:19-20) Sure, God promised He would answer your prayers, but you need to read the rest of the Bible to understand the <u>conditions</u> for having those prayers answered the way you requested. For example: *"...Ye ask, and receive not, because ye ask amiss, that ye may consume it upon your lusts."* (James 4:3)

Don't ask: The other side of asking amiss is not asking at all! People don't ask because they simply don't have the faith that God will grant the request. This is just as dumb as asking for something amiss. It is important to note that often God will not move until He receives a request from us! *"..ye have not because ye ask not.."* (James 4:2) And, remember the verse *"Ask, and it shall be given you; seek, and ye shall find; knock, and it shall be opened unto you:..."* (Matt. 7:7) So ask!

Just examine your motive before you ask! Wouldn't it be sad if you got to Heaven and found out you could have had something if you had only asked? So ask!! But, as indicated above, the key is to ask in God's will and for unselfish reasons.

To impress others: We have all seen those who, when engaged in group prayer, try to pray louder and longer than everyone else. They usually do this to appear more "spiritual" than those around them while in reality they are less spiritual. *"Take heed that ye do not your alms before men, to be seen of them: otherwise ye have no reward of your Father which is in heaven."* (Matt. 6:1)

When praying in group or public prayer, you should **concentrate on being in God's presence and speaking to Him.** Forget what others think. They should be praying instead of listening to you anyway. So, be alone with Him if you want the prayer answered.

Double-mindedness: The Lord wants you to be consistent. He cannot stand a "wishy washy" Christian, who is back and forth, on and off, "hot" and "cold" in their relationship to Him. *"A double-minded man is unstable in all his ways."* (James 1:8) Are you with Him, or against Him? Hot or cold? Make up your mind!

His will not yours: Your prayers should be humble and unselfish petitions to God. It is imperative that we trust Him and His judgment for what is best in our lives. If the Lord gave us everything we asked for, it would be a disaster for us. There are so many things that we cannot see or understand with these "eyes of flesh," while the Lord, in His wisdom and foresight, is looking at the complete picture. He knows what is in the future for you. He's a giving God, but He gives what is best and what pleases Him, not us.

For example: If the Lord refused your prayer to go on a certain trip, you may be disappointed for sure. However, after you learned the plane had crashed and all aboard were killed, your disappointment would turn to joy and praise for Him. The truth is, you should praise Him even if the plane did not crash, because God's will is always perfect. He doesn't make mistakes. You do.

Even Jesus Himself prayed: *"... **Father, if thou be willing, remove this cup from me: <u>nevertheless not my will, but thine, be done</u>.**"* (Luke 22:42) If Jesus was in submission, shouldn't you be?

Finally, don't be afraid to pray. Many are shy about praying and are not sure how to talk to God. Speak to Him in a natural, but sincere tone of voice. Don't pray in some fake voice of extreme reverence to try to seem spiritual to others. That is of the flesh. You must worship God in Spirit and in truth, so your prayer should be a spiritual exchange, not a religious Hollywood sideshow. Speak as you would to your earthly father whom you love and respect. Say what you mean and mean what you say. He does!!

And remember: He is reading your heart like an open book! Be honest, sincere and speak from your heart. *"**Let us therefore come boldly unto the throne of grace, that we may obtain mercy, and find grace to help in time of need.**"* (Heb. 4:16) Believe Him when He says: *"...**Open thy mouth wide, and I will fill it.**"* (Ps. 81:10)

Now that you have read the basic fundamentals of prayer you should be a little better prepared to communicate with God.

Nevertheless, you should remember to ask the Lord to teach you how to pray in a way that is pleasing to Him.

Remember, "practice makes perfect," so bring yourself frequently into His presence and labor to establish a permanent line of communication. Don't be like many modern day Christians and only call on Him when you are in trouble or want something. The Lord desires a constant fellowship with His children. Don't disappoint Him!

If you have reached this point in this book and are still unsaved (or simply not absolutely sure of your salvation) now is the time to use the power of prayer to obtain eternal life through Jesus Christ. Turn to the last page in the book and pray the "sinner's prayer" from your heart. He that suffered, bled and died for your sins, will save you! Do it now! Don't allow the Devil to talk you out of it, or hide the need for it, as he has done before (II Cor. 4:3-4)!

Chapter 12

Giving

"Give, and it shall be given unto you; good measure, pressed down, and shaken together, and running over, shall men give into your bosom. For with the same measure that ye mete withal it shall be measured to you again." Luke 6:38

One of the most profound statements I have ever heard is one heard quite often: *"You cannot out give God."* As often as you hear that repeated you would think people really believed it. However, most Christians' giving habits do not reflect such belief. The leading verse (above) for the chapter pretty much says it all!

Giving is a major fundamental of the Christian life. We are expected to be Christ-like and who could ever "out-give" Him? God desires, and even expects, His children to give, but, He leaves the particulars up to the individual. What size blessing do you want? I have never known a Spirit-filled Christian who was in close fellowship with the Lord who was not "big" on giving. The problem is to get the average Christian to realize that being a generous giver is a blessing and a privilege, not a burden. You are not <u>giving up</u> anything, but rather <u>gaining</u> from the act of giving.

When you mention "giving," most people think only about money, likely because that is the most important thing to them! But remember, giving is not always money. There are many other ways to give including: your time, love, labor, sympathy, wisdom, knowledge, etc. God has promised to give to us as we give.

We are expected to respond to that promise so He can multiply and return it to us (with increase) over and over again. Read the verse again: *"Give, and it shall be given unto you; good measure, pressed down, and shaken together, and running over, shall men give into your bosom. For with the same measure that ye mete withal it shall be measured to you again."* (Lk. 6:38) Do you get the picture?

Now, let's look at some verses under the New Testament Covenant and see how the early Church gave to get a better understanding of the subject. A good place to start is in the book of Acts where we find the early Christians selling what they had to help the poor brethren. *"Neither was there any among them that lacked: for as many as were possessors of lands or houses sold them, and brought the prices of the things that were sold, [35] And laid them down at the apostles' feet: and distribution was made unto every man according as he had need."* (Acts 4:34-35)

Again in Romans 15:26 we find Christians helping their needy brothers in Christ: *"For it hath pleased them of Macedonia and Achaia to make a certain contribution for the poor saints which are at Jerusalem."*

Then in I Corinthians 16:1-2 we find Paul instructing Church Age Saints to give as God had <u>prospered</u> them. Notice that no mention is made of giving a tithe, or "tenth," only to give as God had prospered them. *"Now concerning the collection for the saints, as I have given order to the churches of Galatia, even so do ye. [2] Upon the first day of the week let every one of you lay by him in store, as God hath prospered him, that there be no gatherings when I come."* (I Cor. 16:1-3)

Yet another example of giving is recommended by Paul in II Corinthians 8. In this case it is about people giving back and forth to each other according to the need. *"[8] I speak not by commandment, but by occasion of the forwardness of others, and to prove the sincerity of your love. ...... [13] For I mean not that other men be eased, and ye burdened: [14] But by an equality, that now at this time <u>your abundance may be a supply for their want, that their abundance also may be a supply for your want</u>: that there may be equality:"* (II Cor. 8:8, and 13-14)

Notice Paul said this is not a commandment, but an act proving the sincerity of your love! **Following, are some more verses on the concept of giving in our day:**

Give To Receive
"But this I say, He which soweth sparingly shall reap also sparingly; and he which soweth bountifully shall reap also bountifully. [7] Every man according as he purposeth in his heart, so let him give; not grudgingly, or of necessity: for God loveth a cheerful giver." (II Cor. 9:6-7) We have all been taught

to give and expect nothing in return, but this teaching is not scriptural! <u>God has not only promised to give back if you give, but also, He even promised to return more the more you give! So, you should expect something in return for your giving the same as God expects you to return His giving.</u> **Just don't let receiving be the <u>motive</u> for your giving!**

"Like Kind" Reaping

Another principle in giving and receiving is "like kind" reaping. Most of the time you will reap the same manner of seed you sow. *"Be not deceived; God is not mocked: for whatsoever a man soweth, that shall he also reap."* (Gal. 6:7) Although the context of this verse is primarily dealing with sin, the principle holds true with giving. If you sow corn, you reap corn, sow cucumbers, you reap cucumbers. So it follows that if you sow money you will reap money. If you sow time, you will reap time in return. If you sow love you will reap love, and if you sow the word of God, you will reap souls, etc. Although there are always exceptions to the rule, this is God's universal law. Like the verse says, "you reap what you sow."

Where Do You Give?

Paul told the Church of Corinth to "lay in store" on the first day of the week when the Church met. (I Cor. 16:2) The principle here is giving to the church or ministry where you are being fed the word of God. The pastor or elders are then responsible for using it for God's work as they are led by the Spirit. This is where the bulk of your offerings should go, but not necessarily all of it. There are children's homes, ministries to those incarcerated, rescue missions, missionaries and the poor and needy in your community. With prayer, God will lead you where to place your

132

offerings!

Remember

Although, as a Christian in the "Church Age" you are not under the bondage of the Jewish Law doctrinally. You are instructed to give from the heart as God has prospered you. God loves a cheerful giver and will return and even multiply your reward. Or, you can give nothing and receive nothing in return! It's your responsibility. You will surely reap what you sow!

One last thought on giving. Jesus praised the poor woman who had little, but gave all she had, and indicated her reward was far greater than those who gave more, but without sacrifice. **There is always a bigger blessing and reward for givimg when you can least afford to give it!! And needless to say it will surely augment your efforts toward "walking in the light!"**

Chapter 13

Preparing The Vessel

"If we confess our sins, he is faithful and just to forgive us our sins, and to cleanse us from all unrighteousness." I John 1:9

At this point we have spent considerable time pointing out the things that are deadly to your personal relationship and walk with Him. Not what you expected perhaps, but information necessary to set a course and establish a mind set for *"walking in the Light."*

From those few "fellowship killers" mentioned, you have a picture of what happened to the spiritual condition of the church as a whole. It (the Church) has already fallen to these enemies in a great and ongoing spiritual war. Unfortunately, Bible prophecy does not include any great church revival in this final age, so making it right is an individual thing. It starts with you! But don't expect a lot of company from other Christians wanting to "walk in the light" of His presence.

Regardless of the condition of the church as a whole, you (personally) need to make sure things are right between you and God. Assuming you are still willing to pursue that awesome fellowship with the Creator, this will be the first step. Not knowing the present spiritual condition of the reader, it makes sense to start at the beginning so we don't lose anybody!

Understanding Your Salvation

Christians come in all ages, with diverse backgrounds and various numbers of years as a Christian. However, one thing is common to all, once you were saved, you began as a new creature in Christ Jesus so we'll begin there. It will be of great help for you to take your Bible and read Romans Chapters 6—8 carefully. There is a wealth of related information there.

Notice first, that being saved and "in Christ" means that you become part of His death and resurrection as well!! *"Therefore we are buried with him by baptism into death: that like as Christ was raised up from the dead by the glory of the Father, even so we also should walk in newness of life."* (Rom. 6:4 Underline emphasis ours)

God expects His people to walk in newness of life!! He wants us to live and walk in the new Spirit and not the flesh. *"Therefore if any man be in Christ, he is a new creature: old things are passed away; behold, all things are become new."* (II Cor.5:17) **There are some things that the new man should know**, and be confident in, that will help in his daily walk with God.

Know These Things:

Know that you are saved, and that you have already overcome. (I John 4:4, 5:4) The "old man" died at Calvary. *"I am crucified with Christ: nevertheless I live; yet not I, but Christ liveth in me: and the life which I now live in the flesh I live by the faith of the Son of God, who loved me, and gave himself for me."* (Gal. 2:20)

Know that flesh is dead to sin. You must be confident in your salvation. Understand that the spiritual circumcision in Colossians II (read it) separated the real you, the soul, from the filth of the flesh and sealed your soul unto the day of redemption of the body. (Eph 4:30, and Rom 8:23)

Know that you have put off the old man and that you have put on the new man. (Col. 3:9-10)

OFF THE OLD MAN	ON THE NEW MAN
Adam	Christ
Carnal	Spiritual
Flesh	Spirit

Know that death has no more dominion over us after we are saved according to Rom. 7-10. What a wonderful thing salvation is! God's people never again have to worry about the second death (Hell)!! Understand, however, that sin can separate us from fellowship with God the same way disobedience separates us from our earthly parents. Like God, they may be angry or disappointed, but we still belong to them. Once born into a family you're always a member!! Are you in God's family?

Reckon (depend) **on Christ.** *"Likewise reckon ye also yourselves to be dead indeed unto sin, but alive unto God through Jesus Christ our Lord."* (Rom. 6:11) "To reckon" means "to count on."

Now, you can "reckon" on your new life through Christ knowing you are alive only through Him. **You must understand that you cannot live the Christian life yourself! You must learn to let**

Christ live it through you!

So then, count on Christ and that Spiritual walk with Him because you can't do it by yourself in the flesh. *"So then they that are in the flesh cannot please God."* (Rom. 8:8) It must be done in the Spirit.

".....I can do all things through Christ which strengtheneth me." Phil. 4:13

Your Sins

Knowing these things and being confident of your salvation and a home in Heaven for all eternity, is a wonderful thing to look forward to continually. But, there is still the daily battle. When a Christian sins, those sins are reaped in the flesh. Like the verse says, *"Be not deceived; God is not mocked: for whatsoever a man soweth, that shall he also reap* (Gal. 6:7). Or, *"...be sure your sin will find you out.* (Num. 32:23)

If you sin after you are saved (and every Christian does, I Jn. 1:8) you bring on the chastisement of the Lord (Heb. 12:8). Pay special arttention to those "besetting" sins you have been dealing with on and off since you were saved, but have failed to get complete victory over. The one(s) you keep committing over and over. Yes, those! They have to go, so get started.

These sins separate you from fellowship with God, although they don't affect your salvation because you are "sealed" until the day of redemption (Eph. 4:30). However, there will be no **walking in the light** with unconfessed sin in your life. So how do you deal with this recurring sinful nature of the flesh and get back in fellowship with God?   It is simple, but it must be sincere. The answer is found in the book of I John in the first chapter. This was mentioned earlier, but it's so important we'll address it again.

"This then is the message which we have heard of him, and declare unto you, that God is light, and in him is no darkness at all. [6] If we say that we have fellowship with him, and walk in darkness, we lie, and do not the truth: [7] But if we walk in the light, as he is in the light, we have fellowship one with another, and the blood of Jesus Christ his Son cleanseth us from all sin. [8] If we say that we have no sin, we deceive ourselves, and the truth is not in us. [9] If we confess our sins, he is faithful and just to forgive us our sins, and to cleanse us from all unrighteousness. [10] If we say that we have not sinned, we make him a liar, and his word is not in us."

Confess your sins with a sincere repentance, and He will forgive you. This will remove the sin barrier, thus making way for the restoring of fellowship. Notice He said He would forgive you of all sin. There is nothing of which a Christian cannot be forgiven! However, He did not say that he would remove the punishment. Remember, you reap what you sow! It is a good practice to confess your sin of word, thought or deed, as soon as you realize you have committed it. This way you won't forget it.

For example: A simple and sincere prayer could be: *"Lord, forgive me that sinful thought I just had. Wash and cleanse my mind in your blood and Help me to avoid such sinful thoughts."* Confessing your sins to regain fellowship is only one aspect of prayer that is so important in your Christian life. This is why a whole chapter was devoted to it earlier. Learn how to pray!

Study To Show Thyself Approved

Bible reading and study places the scripture into our hearts and minds for use by the Holy Ghost. David said, *"Thy word have I hid in my heart, that I might not sin aganist thee."* You should heed that advice. The Bible is the living word of the living God, the source of our faith (Rom. 10:17) and a mirror to our souls. God speaks to us and through the scripture instructs us in all matters of faith and practice. You can read it in the flesh and it will do little but put you to sleep.

On the other hand, if you are in sweet fellowship with your Lord (and abiding there) you will consume it as "living water" as God feeds you with its untold riches.

> *Thy word is a lamp unto my feet, and a light unto my path. I have sworn, and I will perform it, that I will keep thy righteous judgments.* Ps. 119:105-106

Christians should realize that God's written word is the bread Of life and can yield great power in their lives if they will receive it in the Spirit. Someone said, *"the Bible is God's love letter to us."* Therefore, we should love it, seek His face through it, glean God's instructions from it and teach it to others as God provides the opportunity. God's living word and our prayers to Him are an awesome combination. A good starting place for study on these subjects would include: II Tim. 2:15, John 5:39, James 5:16, and I Thess. 5:17.

Remember this: the power of prayer and Bible study in your life are directly related to your relationship and nearness to Jesus

Christ. **Everything else will fall in place naturally if you nourish that relationship through these mediums.** It all begins with a mutual love between He and thee; the flesh yielding to the Spirit!!

Serve Him

Jesus gave the great commandment in Matthew 22:37 *"Thou shalt love the Lord thy God with all thy heart, and with all thy soul, and with all thy mind."* It goes without saying that if you really love Him you will want to serve Him and please Him. Therefore the great commission goes hand and hand with that great commandment. The commission is given in Mark 16: *"Go ye into all the world, and preach the gospel to every creature."* (Mark 16:15 See also Acts 1:8.)

Every Christian should be prepared to present the Gospel as opportunity presents itself and, to a large degree, minister as the Apostle Paul admonished young Timothy: *"I charge thee therefore before God, and the Lord Jesus Christ, who shall judge the quick and the dead at his appearing and his kingdom; 2 Preach the word; be instant in season, out of season; reprove, rebuke, exhort with all longsuffering and doctrine."* (II Tim 4:1-2)

The lost world should be able to see Christ in you and be drawn by the hope and faith that radiates from you. Then, when they ask about your faith, you should be quick and ready to give answer! *"But sanctify the Lord God in your hearts: and be ready always to give an answer to every man that asketh you a reason of the hope that is in you with meekness and fear:"* (I Pet. 3:15)

The question often comes up, How much am I expected to do as a Christian? My answer is: How much did He do for you? These next verses serve as a good starting place. *"I beseech you therefore, brethren, by the mercies of God, that ye present your bodies a living sacrifice, holy, acceptable unto God, which is your reasonable service. [2] And be not conformed to this world: but be ye transformed by the renewing of your mind, that ye may prove what is that good, and acceptable, and perfect, will of God. "* (Rom. 12:1-2)

One day, not too far removed, we Christians will all stand before the Judgment Seat of Christ to give an account of our actions and what fruit (if any) we have produced for Him since we were saved. Therefore, let every one of us labor and presevere in the purpose set before us. *"Wherefore seeing we also are compassed about with so great a cloud of witnesses, let us lay aside every weight, and the sin which doth so easily beset us, and let us run with patience the race that is set before us, [2] Looking unto Jesus the author and finisher of our faith; who for the joy that was set before him endured the cross, despising the shame, and is set down at the right hand of the throne of God. "* (Heb. 12:1-2)

We know that all are not called to be a pastor, preacher, missionary or even to some specific work. Nevertheless, all Christians should be able to present the Gospel clearly and should have studied enough Bible (II Tim. 2:15) to explain the fundamentals of the faith. Are you prepared for Him to use you?

Fasting

Fasting (used in concert with prayer) is an awesome weapon in the Christian's arsenal. It is the child of God's "smart weapon" that super charges the power of prayer. With the exception of the written word, fasting and prayer together are an unequaled power in the universe! The Christian invariably benefits both **spiritually** and **physically** by fasting. It simply clears the mind and helps you focus spiritually.

By giving up something our flesh craves, in exchange for Spiritual power from on high, we exhibit to our God the sincerity of our prayers and the desire to draw closer to Him. After only a day or so you will begin to notice a difference in your spirituality, not to mention the fact you will feel better and have more mental energy.

Done properly and sincerely, fasting purges the mind and body of worldliness, thus purifying the vessel and sanctifying it. This prepares you to meet HIM in that special place of fellowship. If you are born again and have never tried prayer and fasting, but desire to experience the fruits of that closeness and the unleashed power of prayer, then try it! While it may take considerable effort and commitment to get started, the experience and rewards will be great. So, with that in mind, let's examine the subject.

Biblical Fasting

In the Bible, a blackslidden Israel seeking forgiveness and desiring to regain fellowship with God, fasted as they prayed confessing their sins. *"Now in the twenty and fourth day of this month the children of Israel were assembled with fasting, and with sackclothes, and earth upon them. And the seed of Israel separated themselves from all strangers, and stood and confessed their sins, and the iniquities of their fathers,"* (Neh. 9:1-2).

In Psalms, David fasted and prayed to fight off those who were intent on his destruction. *"But as for me, when they were sick, my clothing was sackcloth: I humbled my soul with fasting; and my prayer returned into mine own bosom."* (Ps. 35:13) Again David fasted and begged God to deliver him from his enemies and sins: *"When I wept, and chastened my soul with fasting, that was to my reproach."* (Ps. 69:10-14)

Fasting is sometimes necessary for the faith required in dealing with unclean spirits. This was evidenced by Jesus' disciples asking why they could not cast out a certain unclean spirt:

"And Jesus said unto them, Because of your unbelief: for verily I say unto you, If ye have faith as a grain of mustard seed, ye shall say unto this mountain, Remove hence to yonder place; and it shall remove; and nothing shall be impossible unto you. [21] Howbeit this kind goeth not out but by prayer and fasting," (Matt.17:20-21). They had cast out other spirits, but this one was different. It required prayer and fasting to acquire the faith necessary to be successful.

And in yet another case in the Bible, husband and wife are told to fast and pray to bring them back together again: *"Defraud ye not one the other, except it be with consent for a time, that ye may give yourselves to fasting and prayer; and come together again, that Satan tempt you not for your incontinency,"* (I Cor. 7:5).

So, as we study these examples of fasting and prayer in God's written Word, we see that this practice is in order when one needs power from on high and/or God's intervention for anything, including:

143

* **Forgiveness of sins and iniquities**
* **Humbling oneself before God**
* **Chastening oneself in sorrow**
* **Increasing faith**
* **Protection from one's enemies**
* **Domestic problems**

Fasting In Today's Times

When should I fast? Although the above examples are in rather serious situations, you should not wait for some crisis to develop in your life and force you to fast in desperation. Prayer and fasting (with an honest motive of seeking God's face) opens the spiritual doors of your heart. It allows you to more easily hear and recognize His voice as He speaks to you. This is between you and Him. Don't be bragging to everyone like the hypocrites in Mathew 6:16 about what you are doing!

How often should I fast and how long? How often is your need or desire to reach out to Him with a special need; or how often will He call on you to do so? That frequency, along with the time table (duration), and *type* of fast are factors on which you should seek His will. Ask Him! He will guide you.

What are the types of fasting? There are several types of fasting you can try, but there are health considerations such as: Are you on medication? Do you have any health conditions that might be a factor? Again, you should seek God's will on this. Many check with their medical doctor when health issues are involved.

The general idea is to abstain from solid foods. Although some

144

fast without water or solid food for a limited time, this has health risks. I would recommend this only <u>if you know those instructions came from the Lord</u>.

The most common fast is some form of a liquid diet. Liquid is needed to hydrate the body which can go without solid food much longer than without fluids before starting to shut down. You are sacrificing the most desirable food! You could try one of these:

Water only: Use water without chlorine or other chemicals. Distilled water would be a good choice. This is the *real* fast, in the author's opinion.

Fruit & vegetable juice: To me, this is not really a fast, but is an option if health conditions make it necessary. If this is your choice, store bought fruit juices should be 100% juice without sugar etc. Fresh juice with low acid content squeezed immediately before drinking is preferred. Stronger juices can be diluted with water so as not to irritate an empty stomach. Vegetables can be also juiced with a juicing machine.

> *"Moreover when ye fast, be not, as the hypocrites, of a sad countenance: for they disfigure their faces, that they may appear unto men to fast. Verily I say unto you, They have their reward."* Matt. 6:16

Broth: Again, this is another option for health reasons. You can boil potatoes and other vegetables and drink the broth or simply buy some beef or chicken bouillon cubes at the local market. Any of these will furnish some degree of nutrition for the body while still abstaining from solid food.

Getting Started

1. Pray for guidance. You need the Lord's guidance on all factors of fasting.

2. Set A realistic goal. Don't set yourself up for failure with an overly strict a diet or for too long a term initially. The Lord will not direct you to overdo.

3. Cleanse the vessel: Having your sins all confessed up (I Jn. 1:9) and under the blood is a prerequisite to fellowship. Be sure that is the case as you begin fasting and watch that relationship take on new dimensions.

4. Prayer & your Bible: When you think of food or when your body says "I am hungry;" then **pray** instead of eating. **Study** (II Tim. 2:15) your Bible. You will be amazed at the things God will show you while in this enhanced spiritual state.

Seek His face like never before, and He will reveal Himself to you like never before! Ask Him to reveal to you His perfect will for your life and to provide direction toward that goal. Listen, for He <u>will</u> speak! You will find that as the fellowship develops, you will soon recognize His voice and feel His presence more than ever. You see, He has been speaking all along! You just weren't in condition to hear! **Fasting is the best way to begin *your journey of "Seeking His Fellowship!"***

Hopefully, by this point, you have gained a good understanding of **where you are, where you need to go, and what to look out for along the way.** So, with a heart fully prepared to draw closer to the Lord than ever before, and ready to begin a fellowship of **"walking in the Light,"** let's continue.

Chapter 14

Walking in His Light

"But if we walk in the light, as he is in the light, we have fellowship one with another, and the blood of Jesus Christ his Son cleanseth us from all sin." I John 1:7

We are finally to the point where we will try and bring it all together for the reader. The first 13 chapters have been an effort to delineate (and put into proper prespective) the controlling factors synonymous with fellowship and "walking in His light." That was the necessary foundation that brings us to this final chapter.

The purpose of this book, as we stated in the beginning, is to encourage you, the reader, to seek a deeper and more rewarding relationship between you and God than ever before. **This is a task that no one else can accomplish or control but you yourself. As we stated in the beginning, fellowship begins within.** That is where He resides in the child of God.

If you are saved, living clean, and have taken the preceeding chapters (especially the "Fellowship Killers") seriously, and have assimilated the information, then the foundation is in place. You now have the tools to build from there. As there is no magic formula, this final chapter will simply offer some closing steps to point you in the right direction. If you are ready, the Lord is waiting to usher you into that special relationship with Him. Here are some keys, that coupled with what you have already learned, will help make this happen.

Worship Him

Worship is showing an intense love and admiration for the Lord. This can take on many forms. For example, although prayer itself is not worship, <u>the praise portion of your prayer</u> can be a form of worship. God loves to hear from you and desires a fervent heart to heart communication, so use that time to praise him for His holiness and for being such a loving God and Saviour. You should have no trouble finding things for which to worship Him.

God is a Spirit: and they that worship him must worship him in spirit and in truth. John 4:24

As a part of your ongoing fellowship with the Lord, it is vital that you develop a well balanced prayer life. You may want to review that chapter on prayer.

Singing to Him can also be a form of worship, depending on the particular song. *Speaking to yourselves in psalms and hymns and spiritual songs, singing and making melody in your heart to the Lord;* (Eph. 5:19). I believe God loves for us to sing songs that glorify Him and for us to use that as a basis for worship and

149

fellowship. Some people sing in the shower, others while driving and at any number of times and places. It doesn't matter so long as it is a song that honors, glorifies and praises Him. He's not concerned with how well you sing (thank God!), but rather the heart felt motive for your singing.

Quoting scripture that uplifts and glorifies Him is another good way to worship. *"I will praise thee with my whole heart: before the gods will I sing praise unto thee. [2]I will worship toward thy holy temple, and praise thy name for thy lovingkindness and for thy truth: for thou hast magnified thy word above all thy name."* (Ps. 138:1-2)

An abundance of useful scripture for this may be found in the Psalms where David praised God continually. Another example: *"Bless the LORD, O my soul: and all that is within me, bless his holy name. [2] Bless the LORD, O my soul, and forget not all his benefits: [3] Who forgiveth all thine iniquities; who healeth all thy diseases; [4] Who redeemeth thy life from destruction; who crowneth thee with lovingkindness and tender mercies; [5] Who satisfieth thy mouth with good things; so that thy youth is renewed like the eagle's.* (Ps. 103:1-5)

Also, many in the New Testament like: *"Thou art worthy, O Lord, to receive glory and honour and power: for thou hast created all things, and for thy pleasure they are and were created."* (Rev 4:11)

Or *".......and they rest not day and night, saying, Holy, holy, holy, Lord God Almighty, which was, and is, and is to come."* (Rev 4:8)

These are only three examples of ways to worship that you can use to initiate communication and thus fellowship.

Praise Him

Praise Him to others. Praise Him for His holiness, for His goodness and mercy along with all the blessings in your life. **Praise Him for the bad things also, as they are usually character builders and things He has allowed you to experience for a reason. Tell Him you are His and totally surrendered to Him and His will in your life, and then show evidence of that surrender.**

Communicate With Him

One of God's great desires concerning mankind is communication with His people. Your times of worship, prayer, singing and quoting scripture are all forms of communication. Actually, you can carry on a conversation with the Lord. Treat Him as your best friend (which He should be anyway) and confide in Him, question Him, seek His wisdom and guidance.

It's hard for some Christians to realize that He is actually present, inside the believer waiting to communicate on the spiritual level. Let Him lead you. A constant communion and fellowship in the Spirit with us is what our Lord has in mind. Once there, the traditional things take on new meaning, and your efforts for Him flow from a love desire of the Spirit rather than from some traditional religious obligation.

Remember, you are never alone. The Lord covets this personal time with you and wants you to relax and enjoy the peace He brings to the relationship. If this is all done with sincerity and consistency, you will be absolutely amazed at the results! And He will be much pleased.

Seek His Will

Seek His will and guidance for your life and listen closely as He speaks to your heart. Most Christians are better at asking than they are at listening. Don't be one of them. There is no happier Christian than the one living and serving in God's perfect will. **He does have a perfect plan and place for your life, and you need to find that sweet spot He has set aside for you.** Believe it or not, you are special and aside from that place He has for you the fruits of the Spirit will never be manifested in your Christian life to the fullest.

It is not uncommon to find Christians who are spiritually weak, unfulfilled, bitter and even miserable in their Christian lives simply because they are living outside of God's will. Don't let that happen. Seek His will through fellowship.

Fellowship fervently with The One who lives inside. Make this a daily routine, and soon you will hunger for His presence continually. Believe me, He is better company than anything or anyone else with which to occupy your time.

Without this relationship it is easy to drift away and let the Lord become a "spare tire" God. That is, one only pulled out when needed and then returned to some far away place called Heaven until needed again. All God hears from Christians like this are their desires of the flesh! Just praying when you need something, going to church three times a week, and trying to do something for the Lord (when you don't really want to) is not the love relationship God had in mind when He created man. **Again remember you can't live it; He has to live it through you**.

Yield to God

"Neither yield ye your members as instruments of unrighteousness unto sin: but yield yourselves unto God, as those that are alive from the dead, and your members as instruments of righteousness unto God." (Rom. 6:13)

Your whole **body, mind** and **soul,** (along with your will) should be **yielded** to God. To yield is to recognize that God has the right of way in your life, and then to let Him lead the way. Simply put, you must be willing to follow Him in the Spirit rather than to follow your flesh down the road it desires. Believe it or not, you'll be happier following Him!!

If you find yielding to His will a difficult task, seek His help and ask for grace in this matter! Remember, you don't have to shout for Him to hear you as He lives inside!

Once you are *totally* yielded, God will begin to reveal His will for your life. He may simply want you to let Him live the Christian life through you as a testimony to the world. On the other hand, He may call you into some service or ministry. Know this, there is no greater joy this side of Heaven than to know you are serving in His perfect will for your life. The reason so many fail to get there is that they never learn the prerequisites of fellowship from the beginning!

Another thing. To be yielded means lto be living a clean life before God and man. **God will never let His child find**

fellowship, joy and happiness in a life of sin. You can count on that! *"For if ye live after the flesh, ye shall die: but if ye through the Spirit do mortify the deeds of the body, ye shall live."* (Rom. 8:13) *"Let not sin therefore reign in your mortal body, that ye should obey it in the lusts thereof."* (Rom. 6:12)

Yes, you <u>will</u> sin after you are saved, but the verse says not to let it "reign" that is to have supreme authority or "power" over you. If you slip up and sin, *".....we have an advocate with the Father, Jesus Christ the righteous:"* (I John 2:1) See? It's easier, and far more rewarding to simply live for Him from the start.

To get rid of sin that separates you from the Father, you must repent of those sins and confess them to restore that sweet fellowship. Remember, you will likely still be chastised because **"you reap what you sow,"** but at least you are forgiven and back in fellowship with your God!!

* Another Yield: There is another kind of yield that means to "produce." The fruit tree "yields" much fruit. Likewise a Christian "walking in the Spirit," will naturally bear fruit for the Saviour. (Rom. 6:22) *"But now being made free from sin, and become servants to God, ye have your fruit unto holiness, and the end everlasting life."* Paul said; *"...but I desire fruit that may abound to your account."* (Phil. 4:17)

If you are walking in the Spirit daily, lost people will see Christ in you and will be drawn to the Saviour because they desire the same love, joy, peace, confidence and happiness they see in your life. These attributes I saw in Christians were instrumental in bringing me to Christ many years ago.

Naturally, you should be busy spreading the Gospel to win souls, but **many may be won or lost simply by your testimony and the life you live before the world.** So, be aware that the lost are watching. And remember, your life can produce a great "yield" of souls for the Lord Jesus if you will simply "walk the walk."

Jesus said to lay up for yourselves treasures in Heaven because where your treasure is, there will your heart be also (Matt. 6:21). Those things that we do for Christ are eternal and will last forever, while the things of this earth (including all of our prized possesions) will all burn up one day. (II Pet. 3:10) Look at it this way: **Your life will soon be past, only what's done for Christ will last!**

Remember, He is an indwelling Spirit that lives within. Seek Him there.

So serve Him well.... and be careful to do it because you love Him, not because you think you must.

Fellowship With Him

Fellowship is defined as "companionship." A friendly association of those sharing common interest. We all have enjoyed fellowship with our loved ones and special friends from time to time. Some of these relations are often life long and can be extremely comforting and gratifying. We love and enjoy them because they love us in return. But, how could anything compare to fellowship with the Creator of the universe, our Lord and Savior who gave His life for us? This is the ultimate relationship we have endevored to convey in these pages. Let's examine the inner workings of "Seeking His Fellowship."

Although somewhat redundant, we will review the daily walk and it's significance. Your day should begin with prayer and Bible study. The Bible must be your final authority in all matters of faith and practice. As you progress through the day, walk in complete submission and fellowship with God as you go about your day in His presence.

This means including Him and making Him a partner in all aspects of your daily life. Don't discard Him with the customary "Amen" after a morning prayer, but rather take Him with you all day, imagining Him at your side at all times. He's there (actually inside)! So talk to Him! Naturally, He is always there but this communication will make **you** more aware of that presence.

This awareness fosters a spiritual nearness, manifested through His passionate love for us and our returning that love for Him in a heartfelt fellowship. Believe me, this will affect how you live your life! In it's fullest form it can bring a calmness to the soul, an unshakable faith and a oneness with God never before experienced. It is a point once reached, one never wants to leave. It is as near to Heaven on earth as you will ever reach.

This is a big step from the Sunday and Wednesday church experience that most Christians are content with, not realizing that it is only *part* of the total package.

Although many sincere and godly Christians spend their whole lives trying to achieve this close fellowship with God through the religious traditions of ritualistic prayer, reading the Bible and going to church, it can't be reached from there alone. God's people often must force themselves to do these things, finding little joy or fulfillment from them and never understanding why.

To be honest, haven't there been times when you realized you were just going through the motions although your heart was not really into praying or going to church? Haven't there been times that it was just out of a feeling of obligation that you did so? I mean.....*"it's the right thing to do so we have to do it"* Isn't that the feeling of many? Have you "been there and felt that?"

What is wrong in these cases? Assuming it's not your church, (and it may be, at least partially) it's most likely a lack of a close personal relationship with the Savior on your part! Many expect their pastor to do it all. It doesn't work that way! This is one of those things you have to seek and accomplish for yourself! So get busy if you fall into that category!

Then, on the other hand, some have had such a relationship before and it grew cold because they were too busy "serving." That's right. **You can be so busy so fervently serving the Lord in some ministry trying to get all the work done (to please the Lord) there is no time left for fellowship with the Lord.** Which obviously should have come first anyway.

A good example of this is the two sisters in Luke 10:38-42. One was busy <u>serving</u> the Lord and the other was spending her time <u>worshipping and fellowshipping</u> with Him. Were they both meaningful? Of course! But guess which one the Lord counted as the most important? Read the story.

Another example of this is the

Labor in the Spirit and not in the flesh

authors' own experience. As a detention facility Chaplain some twenty years ago, I was litterly swamped with work. There was preaching, counseling, Bible course tests to grade, new lessons, Bibles, tracts and other materials to be addressed labeled and recorded in the record books. I labored to deliver everything each day so the inmates could get their material as quickly as possible.

When it got to the point I could not finish all this during working hours, I took work home and enlisted my wife's help with the work. Although it was somewhat stressfull, I was proud of my labors because, after all, I was doing it all for the Lord and knew my efforts pleased Him. Right? Wrong!

When it finally got impossible to keep up, in desperation I went to the Lord in prayer seeking help. It wasn't that I hadn't been praying before, but the prayers were hindered from the status of my fellowship. I simply didn't have time to fellowship with the Lord for trying to get all the work out! I had the "cart before the horse" so to speak! So, the Lord let me struggle so I could learn the lesson. Finally, I asked Him for help.

Let me explain the heart-felt reply I got from the Lord. Although I was working as hard as I could to get things done for Him, my labors were all in the **energy of my own flesh** and the results, though admirable at first glance, were only a fraction of what they would have been had I been working in the **energy of the Spirit**. As I was beginning to grow in this respect, my brother came back from the mission field and helped me a great deal in understanding this need to let God work through me. So my experience taught me that sometimes it is necessary to slow down or even temporarly stop the *physical* works we are doing for Him, and have a heart meeting in the *Spirit*!

The secret to a close and ongoing fellowship is to be <u>filled</u> with the Holy Spirit. You say, "well everyone who is saved is in dwelled with the Holy Spirit." True, but being <u>indwelled</u> is not the same as being <u>filled</u>! We all know people who are born again Christians that give no indication of being filled with the Spirit. Face it, **you can be saved and have the Spirit of God, but not be filled with, and walking in that Spirit!**

I once saw a perfect picture of this as I sat watching the flames of a roaring fire through the glass in our wood stove. I was thinking of the tremendous power of that fire as it roared as the long powerful flames licked at the glass.

Then my wife came in (it was getting hot) and closed the air damper off to that fire. As I watched, without air, those powerful flames quickly died to simply a glowing bed of coals, with only an ocassional small flicker of flame. There was still fire in the stove, but the *power* and *ability* to burn freely was gone.

At that point the Lord revealed a great lesson to me. I arose, walked to the stove, and opened the air vent. The weakened (but still alive) fire was hungry and sucked the air that naturally came rushing in like a mighty wind! The flames quickly sprung up again licking powerfully at the glass and roof of the stove. Once again I had a strong and roaring fire!   A stove filled with air was the source of the fire's power! Little air.....little or no power!

Christians get their power from the Holy Ghost (Acts 1:8). Accordingly, your power in Christ is **mighty** when you are <u>filled</u> with that Holy Ghost, yet **weak** and unproductive spiritually when less than filled.

> *But ye shall receive power, after that the Holy Ghost is come upon you: and ye shall be witnesses unto me both in Jerusalem, and in all Judaea, and in Samaria, and unto the uttermost part of the earth.* Acts 1:8

So, when you realize something in your life is restricting your source of power (God's Holy Ghost) in Christ, it's time to get on your knees and get that something confessed and "under the blood." Then the Spirit will enter in like "a rushing mighty wind!" Power is restored and the fruits of the Spirit of God will abound!

> *"For ye were sometimes darkness, but now are ye light in the Lord: walk as children of light:"* Eph 5:8

While being filled with the Holy Spirit can come quickly with repentance and confession, remaining filled is a different matter. It will not come without commitment and consistancy, as I mentioned earlier. **It will come by seeking His presence and applying the many faces of fellowship in your daily life. Each aspect is important: a commitment to study His Book, a surrendered life, separation from the world, crucifying the flesh daily, a**

160

strong prayer life, fellowship with the brethren and more. I'd like to summerize it by saying; push everything else aside and move the Lord Jesus Christ to the forefront of your life. Saturate yourself with Him!

Believe me, that commitment will be the beginning of an ever growing and fruitful fellowship with Him. In other words, it gets better and better as you grow and follow the light!

So there it is! Being filled with the Holy Spirit is necessary for that <u>close personal relationship</u>. The two are synonymous. With that on going fellowship and communion with the Lord Jesus Christ, He is able to work <u>through you</u> in accordance with <u>His</u> will. The end result is amazing! Prayer is no longer a chore but becomes a meaningful part of that union. The spirit now hungers for God's word, and fellowship with the saints at church is something you look forward to, and it's not just an obligation! **Now God's in it! He's living the Christian life through you!**

In order to maintain this spirtual walk, you must crucify the flesh daily to push the world out and keep it out! He simply wants to be an active part of your daily life with the Holy Spirit guiding every step of the way. So, include Him! Seek His advice, companionship and presence in your daily routine. This, of course, takes practice, but you can do it! **Practice the presence of God!** Understand that He wants all of you and that you can't live with your heart and affections set on things of this world and still please God.

He wants to be your first love and be number one in your heart. You should want that same relationship. When it happens the

Lord will really begin to reveal Himself to you like never before. Then, and only then, will the fruits of the Spirit: the love, joy, peace, happiness and other fruits and blessings manifest themselves in the believer's life.

In His Light

> *But as he which hath called you is holy, so be ye holy in all manner of conversation; Because it is written, Be ye holy; for I am holy.* I Peter 1:15-16

"Walking in His Light" is to be on top of the mountian. It is like a small preview of what lies ahead in Heaven. There is nothing this side of Heaven any closer to pure joy than knowing that you are living in His will and experiencing His voice speaking to your heart as He guides you daily in life's decisions. Your faith will abound above what you thought possible, and your confidence in His directing voice will assure that you never want to be without it again!

But, as wonderful of an experience as it can be, it is hard to stay on top of that mountian in light of what you face every day in the world. As your relationship with the Lord grows and moves to greater heights, you will find new challenges from both the Christian and the secular world (as well as within) to interefer with your quest to remain on the top.

Do not be discouraged when you cannot maintain a perfect fellowship all of the time. However, strive for it! It is all but impossible in this world which we must navigate through daily. If it is, in fact possible, you would likely have to be a recluse to acheive that goal. While complete separation from the world and other people might make it easier for you to maintain that "top of the mountain" fellowship with the Lord, it would be contrary to scripture. You would have to lay down the charge Christians are given to witness, to serve and to live as a testimony to the world.

So, if you fall, get back up, get the problems "under the Blood," and seek Him again, knowing that the time will soon come when the fellowship will be face to face in person with Jesus Himself!

Remember These Things:

If ye then be risen with Christ, seek those things which are above, where Christ sitteth on the right hand of God. [2] Set your affection on things above, not on things on the earth. [3] For ye are dead, and your life is hid with Christ in God. [4] When Christ, who is our life, shall appear, then shall ye also appear with him in glory. Col 3:1-4

* **Know** you're saved - be confident in your salvation. Reckon on Jesus to keep you.

* **Communicate** with God. That is where it begins.

* **Yield** to God and He will shape your life.

* **Worship and Praise** through prayer, song and scripture. God is listening.

* **Bible** study is a must! " Study to show thyself approved unto God."

* **Fellowship** with God. It is His heart's desire.

* **Labor** and He will produce fruit that your yield for Christ will be great.

* **Enjoy** your salvation and communion with Him.

* **Follow** the Light. In Him, there is no darkness.

And if life still sometimes seems hard, remember what Paul said; **"For I reckon that the sufferings of this present time are not worthy to be compared with the glory which shall be revealed in us."** (Rom. 8:18)

So, rest in the Lord Jesus Christ knowing the best is yet to come. May your journey be rewarding, may God richly bless you as you **"Seek His fellowship,"** and may His coming be soon. Amen!

REVIEWING WITH
POINTS TO PONDER

Chapter 1   The Desire Of God's Heart

*   *What does it mean to you knowing that God wants to fellowship with you personally?*

*   *What do you feel are the changes necessary in your life for a closer "walk" with the Lord?*

*   *Have you ever experienced a close fellowship with God? If so, how has it affected your Christian life ?*

Chapter 2   What Went Wrong

*   *Were you aware of God's opinion regarding the spiritual condition of today's church as a whole? (Rev. 3:13-18)*

*   *What do you believe is the most obvious weaknesses in today's churches?*

*   *What changes are necessary from today's "norm" for a church to get back in the center of God's will?*

Chapter 3   Knowing God Better

*   *Which of God's many attributes do you consider the most important four to you?*

*   *Can you name four attributes that are not listed?*

*   *What are some of the many names for Jesus found in the Bible?*

Chapter 4   False Doctrine

* Consider, in depth, Paul's charge to the Galatians in Chapter 1:8-9. With respect to the many different denominational teachings on salvation, it will be very revealing for those seeking the truth. Compare these with the true gospel in I Cor. 15:1-4.

* Consider the greatest danger false doctrine presents to the unsaved. What about the dangers those who get involved in false doctrine after salvation?

Chapter 5   Worldliness

* What are the most prevalent influnces of worldliness the Christian faces daily in today's society?

* Which of these give you the most problems personally?

* Do you believe you can overcome these with God's help?

Chapter 6   The Flesh

* How can the Christian best deal with the daily temptations in this life?

* What was /is the greatest temptation for you to overcome since you have been saved?

* Do you ever consider the cost of disobedience before you knowingly do something that displeases God?

Chapter 7   The Devil

* What trait was the devil's downfall and how can this same trait affect a Christian?

* What are the devil's most unholy attributes?

* What is his greatest desire? See Isaiah 14, Ezekiel 28

Chapter 8   Addictions

* How can addictions be best dealt with? Minimized?

* What is the best way to eliminate illegal drugs from our society?

* Do you have any experience with overcoming addictions or drugs?

Chapter 9   Imaginations And Fantasies

* Describe the importance of Christians controlling their imaginations and fantasies.

* What are some precautions a Christian can take to keep such thoughts from entering the mind?

* If unclean thoughts do come to mind, how should they be dealt with?

Chapter 10 Separation
* *How should a backslid brother or sister in Christ be dealt with according to the Bible?*

* *How about with unsaved people?*

* *A good discussion would be, what constitutes fellowship, especially with respect to ministering to these groups.*

Chapter 11 Growing with Prayer
* *Given the awesome power of prayer, why is it not more of a priority in most Christians lives?*

* *Why is the structure or order of one's prayer important?*

* *Who should prayers be directed to?*

Chapter 12 Giving
* *Why is giving so important for the Christian?*

* *Consider the many different ways to give and the related sacrifice with each.*

* *Where or who should your giving be directed to?*

Chapter 13 Preparing The Vessel
* *Preparing the vessel for fellowship has many facets. One of the most important being your understanding and confidence*

in your own salvation. If this is the case with you, on what do you base this confidence? Can you convey this confidence to your lost acquaintances?

Chapter 14 Walking In The Light

*   How do you feel walking in the light of His fellowship will change your Christian life? How about those around you?

*   We always focus on the joy and satisfaction of a close relationship with the Lord, but what about the resulting power it brings to your Christian labors?

*   Have you already made the commitment to pursue that close fellowship with the Lord?

Be Sure Of Your Salvation

If you are not absolutely sure that you are saved, take care of it now!

Jesus said: *"...Ye Must be born again."* (John.3:7)   The Bible says, *"....behold, now is the day of salvation....."* (II Cor. 6:2) God made it easy if you are sincere.

COME NOW JUST AS YOU ARE! A SINNER: "Lord, I know I have sinned against you."

COME WITH A REPENTANT HEART: "Lord, the best way I know how, I now turn away from my sins and seek the righteousness of Jesus Christ."

COME RECEIVING JESUS AS YOUR LORD AND SAVIOUR : "Lord, I believe in my heart, and now confess with my mouth that Jesus died for my sins, that He rose from the dead, and that His shed blood alone is ample and full payment for all my sins. On that basis, I now receive Jesus as my Lord and Saviour. Thank you Lord God for saving my soul."

Can you pray those words and mean them with all your heart ? If you can, and did, then **the Holy Spirit came down and spiritually circumcised you, baptizing you with His Holy Spirit.**   (Col 2:10-14, I Cor 12:13)

Now you can know for sure that you are saved! *"And this is the record, that God hath given to us eternal life, and this life is in his Son. [12] He that hath the Son hath life; and he that hath not the Son of God hath not life. [13] These things have I written unto you that believe on the name of the Son of God; that ye may know that ye have eternal life, and that ye may believe on the name of the Son of God."*